The Little Red Book

TEACHING ESL IN CHINA

Susan Black and *Frank Black*

Order this book online at www.trafford.com/07-2678
or email orders@trafford.com

Most Trafford titles are also available at major online book retailers.

© Copyright 2008 Susan Black and Frank Black.
All rights reserved. No part of this publication may be reproduced, stored in a retrieval system, or transmitted, in any form or by any means, electronic, mechanical, photocopying, recording, or otherwise, without the written prior permission of the author.

Illustrated and Cover Design / Artwork by: Frank Black
Edited by: Elaine Spencer and Lori King
Computer Graphics by: Ashley B. Porter

Note for Librarians: A cataloguing record for this book is available from Library and Archives Canada at www.collectionscanada.ca/amicus/index-e.html

ISBN: 978-1-4251-5915-3

We at Trafford believe that it is the responsibility of us all, as both individuals and corporations, to make choices that are environmentally and socially sound. You, in turn, are supporting this responsible conduct each time you purchase a Trafford book, or make use of our publishing services. To find out how you are helping, please visit www.trafford.com/responsiblepublishing.html

Our mission is to efficiently provide the world's finest, most comprehensive book publishing service, enabling every author to experience success. To find out how to publish your book, your way, and have it available worldwide, visit us online at www.trafford.com/10510

 www.trafford.com

North America & international
toll-free: 1 888 232 4444 (USA & Canada)
phone: 250 383 6864 ♦ fax: 250 383 6804 ♦ email: info@trafford.com

The United Kingdom & Europe
phone: +44 (0)1865 722 113 ♦ local rate: 0845 230 9601
facsimile: +44 (0)1865 722 868 ♦ email: info.uk@trafford.com

10 9 8 7 6 5 4 3 2 1

ABOUT THE AUTHORS

Susan, born in Sudbury, Ontario, and Frank, born in Vancouver, British Columbia, Canada, met and married fifty years later in Port McNeill, a small town on North Vancouver Island. Susan, the computer software trainer, and Frank, the town gardener for Port McNeill, spent their first year together on Frank's twelve metre sailboat.

New life and new dreams drove them to get TESOL certified through Global TESOL College. To kick off teaching English as a second other language, they held classes at the local North Island College instructing students from all parts of the world. They chose China as an overseas destination. Why China? It was the chance to introduce the Bahai Faith as pioneers and they'd never been there. Both having come from varied backgrounds and having had many career changes, adding one more seemed an easy decision.

Frank, an experienced Bahai travel teacher, free-hand sketch artist, carver, and amateur actor, added music to his many interests and uses these talents to teach in China.

Susan, a graduate of DeVry Institute of Technology, holds a Bachelor of Science Degree and a Certificate in Adult Continuing Education. Her long history of teaching provides her the confidence to partner with her husband to develop this book. Frank and Susan Black live and teach in China.

The Little Red Book

TEACHING ESL IN CHINA

Susan Black and *Frank Black*

We wish to dedicate this book to our parents, Armand and Cecile Regimbal, and Andrew and Francis Black, the people who helped us get on the road of life.

And

To our many dear Chinese friends who always gave of their time to assist us in our learning experience in China.

Introduction

In every classroom in every senior middle school in China there is a leader known as the Teacher. There is also a Monitor, several Group Leaders, Subject Study Leaders including an English Study Leader, a Student on Duty, a Classroom Observer and, if you're lucky, a Computer Study Leader. The classroom in China is firmly structured and follows the communist philosophy of duty.

This book reveals the structure of the senior middle school classroom in China and also the traits of students in those classrooms. You will gain credible insight into the duties and responsibilities of the students including what students believe about learning a foreign language and how TESOL teachers fit into the top-heavy bureaucratic school system in China. TESOL stands for Teaching English as a Second Other Language. It can also stand for treating every student out of love. The students are your primary target market and knowing who they are will provide you the confidence to deal with every scenario tossed your way.

The Little Red Book Teaching ESL in China also lays out an exclusive lesson plan on teaching group work to students in China; *a phenomenon that has been thoroughly researched but never enacted* says Mr. Chen, a professor at the School of Foreign Studies, South China Normal University in Beijing. *The Little Red Book* presents a story titled Communism in the Classroom, but the book is not about communism, it's about how the communist system dictates the structure in the Chinese classroom. It has to do with the specific duties of students and the student culture in a typical Chinese senior middle school and how knowing the classroom culture and the roles of the students can help you become a true foreign expert. The structured philosophy of Chairman Mao Tse Tung, the former leader of the People's Republic of China, is alive in the Chinese classroom and that structure and philosophy affects your job as a teacher in China. *The Little Red Book* introduces you to the students whose duty it is to observe and report on the conduct of other students and you, their teacher. You'll also meet a selection of English teachers, including a native speaker who makes a midnight run, and a Chinese English teacher who wishes she could.

Table of Contents

I	**Who's Who in the Chinese Classroom?**	15
	The Teacher According to Confucius	16
	The Teacher According to Students	17
	The Monitor	19
	The Group Leader	20
	The English Study Leader	21
	The Student on Duty	22
	The Classroom Observer	22
	The Computer Leader	23
II	**An Intimate Look at Chinese Students**	25
	Open Forum with Seventy-Three Students	25
	Student Secrets Revealed	27
	Motivators to Learn English	28
III	**What Chinese Students Believe About Learning English**	33
	Questions, Answers and Simple Analysis	33

IV	The International Co-operative Class	43
	Prisoners of the InternationalCo-operative Class 47	

V	For Your Information	53
	A Breakthrough in Culture Shock.. 53	
	Banking at the Bank of China 54	
	Four Essentials for China Post 55	
	What is a Number One School? 56	
	How to Be a Ready, Willing and Able Foreign Teacher 57	

VI	Confessions from China	59
	The Midnight Runner 59	
	The Consequence of Truth 62	
	Communism in the Classroom 64	
	Please Forgive Them, For They Know Not What They Do 65	
	From the Journal of a TESOL Teacher 68	
	The F*** You Message 77	
	Purged in China 78	

VII Teaching Group Work in China:
   A Real-Life Lesson Plan   85
   Group Work is the Work of the Devil.. 89
   What is a Group?... 90
   Your Job as Project Manager.. 90
   Teaching Group Work Instructions 91
   The Structure of a Five Member Group 95
   Group Work Lesson Plan 97

Bibliography   103

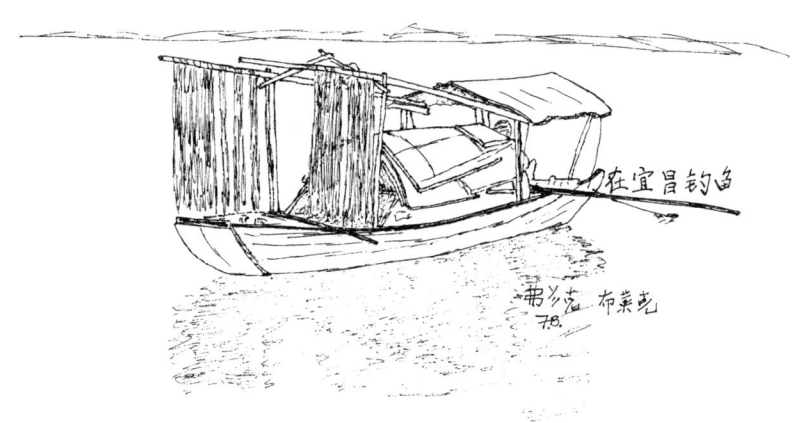

Fishing in Yichang

Who's Who in the Chinese Classroom?

> From the Son of Heaven down the mass of the people, all must consider the cultivation of the person the root of everything besides.
> - *Confucius*

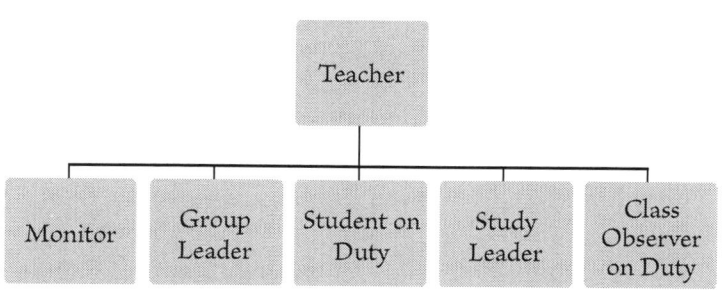

Figure 1 Structure of the classroom in China

THE TEACHER ACCORDING TO CONFUCIUS

The Teacher in China is still a respected individual held over from the ancient Confucius philosophy days. In the history of Chinese education, Confucius was the exemplary model of all teachers, symbolizing his dictum, *educate all without discrimination, and teach according to the abilities of one's students*. Using the six arts of rites, music, archery, chariot driving, learning (including reading and writing), and mathematics, Confucius had more than three thousand disciples during his lifetime. In practice of his philosophy, the Sage never refused a student because of his class or character, requiring only that his pupils possess a sincere desire to learn.

During the crisis of the Spring and Autumn Period, Confucius sought to end the chaos of the times. Believing this disorder to be a reflection of declining morals in society, he carefully toured the various warring Chinese states to advise rulers and officials on the merits of ethical rule. In his later years, Confucius reorganized the ancient Chinese texts, thus laying a solid foundation for China's enduring civilization. In 1939 the Ministry of Education marked that Confucius' birthday would be celebrated on August 28, and designated it as Teachers' Day as well as a national holiday to remember Confucius' enormous contribution to Chinese culture and society. The date was changed to September 28 in 1952 in accordance with chronologists' new findings and then changed again to September 10. Today, Teachers' Day not only honours Confucius but also celebrates all teachers for their hard work during the year.

Every year during Teachers' Day, the Confucius Memorial Service is held at the Confucius Temple, located in his hometown in present-day Chufu, Shantung Province, to show respect and honour for the wise man. At the Teachers' Day Celebration held by the Ministry of Education and the various local governments, teachers with the highest seniority and best qualities are recognized for their contribution to society.

Phyllis Ghim Lian Chew, in <u>The Chinese Religion and the Baha'i Faith</u>, says "Confucius' time was a non-technological era without the convenience of mass communication. Thus, the imitation of models was the easiest and simplest form of learning. An important part of the teacher's role was to act as a model himself and to provide an example of what the moral human being should be like."

This ancient philosophy is like the more recent Baha'i faith values, where education is greatly emphasized and encouraged. In <u>Tablets</u>, Baha'u'llah, the faith's Most Holy Teacher says, "Knowledge is as wings to man's life, and a ladder for his ascent. Its acquisition is incumbent upon everyone."

In a disappointing downturn, the respect that the Chinese had for teachers was destroyed both by the Communist takeover of China in 1949 and by western influential takeover of the education system. In political campaigns during the Cultural Revolution, for example, intellectuals were often the target of maltreatment and teachers suffered at the hands of their students. The more recent upswing momentum comes from the students themselves who, in their own words, express an admiration for teachers who deserve the praise.

THE TEACHER ACCORDING TO STUDENTS

According to 1,156 grade one, two and three senior middle school students in China, a teacher, whether Chinese or foreign, should be kind above all else. The students filled in a graphic organizer like the one below to express their ideas of what *the best teacher* should be and the results generated these descriptors. Grade one, two and three senior middle school students are equivalent in age to Grade 10, 11 and 12 high school students in Canada. According to the students, the best teacher has the following uncomplicated characteristics: beautiful, funny, kind, pleasant, strong and wonderful. Below are student revelations about their best teacher.

> *My best teacher is Long Tang. Because he's very friendly and he very likes to forget. Some things we can't forget but he says forget. If we are a little or a lot sad he says forget. I like him very much. He likes words. I like how the words feel. It's very nice. He told us a lot of things. He made me happy. He made me don't cry. He is unique.* Yang Yang

> *There are so many good teachers in my high school that I can't choose. They are kind, careful and friendly. I like them. They can smile at everybody, especially Mrs. Black. When I was ill, they help me to the hospital.* Danni Huang

> *Yang Qi Tao is our P.E. teacher so he is healthy and freer than the others teachers. He is kind fabulous and pleased, he give us a free time in class, he is the only teacher let us play sports in class. So, I like him.* Xi Hu

The students also expressed that they don't like it when a teacher brutally chastises them in front of the other members of the class, or when they are slapped across the face, or when they are singled out to speak in front of the class, or, like any other student anywhere in the world, to be treated unfairly. Something interesting that some of the students admitted they didn't like, is the rule enforced by the Chinese school administrators that they mustn't fraternize with students of the opposite sex. They said they are allowed to make friends with boys or girls, but they must keep their distance. When asked how she feels about it, Sun Jia Li, a 17-year-old, in grade three said "it must be because it is impossible to have a boyfriend because it affects our studies. You can make friends with boys. It's OK." The general tendency of most students is not to admit that they don't like something. The tendency is to go with the flow.

THE MONITOR

The classroom in China is firmly controlled by the communist system and follows the communist philosophy of obligation. One of the system's strongest advocates of duty and teacher support is the classroom Monitor. Meet classroom Monitor Yue Yu, a grade two student in a senior middle school in Yichang, Hubei province. Grade two in China can be compared to grade eleven in Canada. Yue Yu's duty as Monitor is to observe and report the overall conduct of the students to the Head Teacher. The Monitor is also responsible for reporting on the conduct of the teacher, English or otherwise. Yue Yu dutifully reports student and teacher absence, misbehaviour, inappropriate language, inappropriate topics, late arrival, unfinished homework and homework not handed in. Yue Yu takes her duties as Monitor very seriously.

"Yue Yu, how did you get chosen to be class Monitor?"

"The Head Teacher chose me as Monitor because I have high marks in every subject."

Yue Yu's English is a band score of 4 IELTS. IELTS stands for International English Language Testing System. It is a test of English language skills designed for students who want to study in the medium of English either at university, college or senior middle school. Yue Yu's band score of four indicates that she is a limited user and that she has *basic* English language competence that is limited to familiar situations. Yue Yu has frequent problems in understanding and expression and is not able to use complex language. This is good news and bad news for the English teacher, because part of Yue Yu's responsibility is to report your words and actions in the classroom to the Head Teacher and you want her to comprehend your meaning. It is common that you're watched and reported on everywhere you go in China. Yue Yu is not wearing the distinctive burgundy armband worn by the street-corner observation representative in China, but in her role as classroom Monitor she might as well be. The duty of classroom Monitor is described by Peng Wen Juan, a Chinese English teacher, this way:

> *In my opinion, the job of the monitor in a class is to be a good example and a good guide, to lead the class to having a good attitude towards studying, and also help teachers to have good classes.*

To paraphrase a quote from Mao Tse Tung, "if you want to know the taste of a pear, you must change the pear by eating it yourself. If you want to know the structure of the classroom in China, you must take part in teaching English as a second language in China. All genuine knowledge originates in direct experience."

THE GROUP LEADER

You will recognize the Group Leader once the students are seated. He's the first student in each row. The number of Group Leaders you have available to you depends on the number of rows you have in your classroom. The primary duty of the Group Leader is to collect the homework or in-class assignment from each student in the row, and then hand the work over to the teacher. They can also help the teacher hand back any student work. The Group Leader will dutifully follow your instruction to distribute student handouts or whatever you've got going on. Your enthusiastic thank-you goes a long way in maintaining the Group Leader's support and cooperation.

> *If the only prayer you ever say in your life is 'thank-you,' it will be enough.*
> *- Meister Eckhart*

THE ENGLISH STUDY LEADER

There are as many Study Leaders in your classroom as there are subjects to study. The student that you want to pay special attention to is the English Study Leader. Here's how Pei Min, a Chinese English teacher describes the duty of an English Study Leader:

> I'm very glad to give you some information about the duty of an English study leader. As a study leader, her duty is to help the teacher finish the teaching task. For example, she ought to hand in and hand out the exercise books or papers. And she ought to reflect some information about the opinions and study of the students to the teacher. To become the link between the teacher and the students. Meanwhile you can give her some work to help you in teaching or activities in class.

Meet Fly, the English Study Leader in Class 14, Grade One. His Chinese name is Cheng Fei Xiang, and he conducts himself as English Study Leader with pride.

"Please tell me about your duties as English Study Leader, Fly."

"I help all the other students with their English studies."

"And what things do you do to help them?"

"When we have English study time, I make sure the other students study well."

"How do you do that?"

"I help the students write down the English words."

"And then what do you do?"

"I help them say the English words."

Fly's actions are a living display of the writings of Confucius who said "it is pointless to learn merely for the sake of learning. Application must be the end and learning the means." Confucius puts great emphasis on the relationship between knowledge and action. The Chinese believe that it is education which has been responsible for the ascent of mankind and progress in society. Given an opportunity, every student is a teacher.

THE STUDENT ON DUTY

The job assigned to the Student on Duty in a classroom is to keep the classroom tidy including erase the blackboards, sweep the floor, and align the desks and other such clean up duties. The student on duty who performs these daily clean-up tasks changes each day, but if you ask who is on duty the response generally includes other students pointing out the young person, and him then standing waiting for your direction.

THE CLASSROOM OBSERVER

Wang Jie Yu is a pretty young girl who stands just inside the classroom holding a clipboard that shields an elaborate form. She is wearing the mandated school uniform as a distinction that she is on duty. A chime sounds that indicates the end of a class and the beginning of the eye exercise program. Feng Yafang, a colleague, explains "it's a government directive. All full-time schools across China have to do this same eye exercise routine to stay healthy." The eye exercises involve rubbing over, under and on the eyes to a count of six sets of eight. The count bellows out in true military style through the school's public announcement system while lilting music plays in the background. The classroom I'm standing in holds three teacher-appointed exercise monitors, a position coveted by those who walk around the class throughout the exercise routine keeping a severe eye on the student body to make sure everyone is doing the exercises and if there is a lapse, to punish the erring student by whispering chastising words.

"Everybody across China does the same exercise for at least twelve years of his or her academic life. I remember doing the exercise when I was a young girl in primary school, and I just hated it," says Feng Yafang.

For ten minutes every morning, at precisely 11:25 a.m., Wang Jie Yu and countless other Classroom Observers across China are scrutinizing the conduct of the student body, the performance of the exercise monitors, and the cleanliness of the classroom. Their observations are recorded on an official school form, signed-off by the classroom Monitor and then whisked away by the Classroom Observer, who dutifully delivers the precious document to the Head Teacher.

THE COMPUTER LEADER

If you're lucky enough to have multimedia capability in your classroom, then you'll be lucky enough to have a computer leader to assist you. Even if you're fluent in reading Chinese characters or have memorized all the dropdown and context menus, the duty of the computer leader in your classroom is to assist the teacher and it's a responsibility the student generally looks forward to. This gives you prime opportunity to communicate one-on-one with your computer leader as she manipulates the electronics to enhance your class performance.

In every school in China you are surrounded by thousands of students performing their specific duties. The most important thing you can do is to recognize the existence of the classroom monitor, group leaders, student on duty, classroom observer, and subject leaders, and to learn about them, their task, their dedication to that duty and to you. They are trained to perform to the best of their ability and doing so gives them a personal sense of pride and also puts them in good favour with school teachers and administrators. It also gives the student a strong sense of belonging. Knowing who your students are and what they do will contribute greatly to the smooth operation of your classroom.

> *Learning takes place when one is able to enact social norms after having learnt them. A 'transformation' effected in a practical action must take place.*
> *- Confucius*

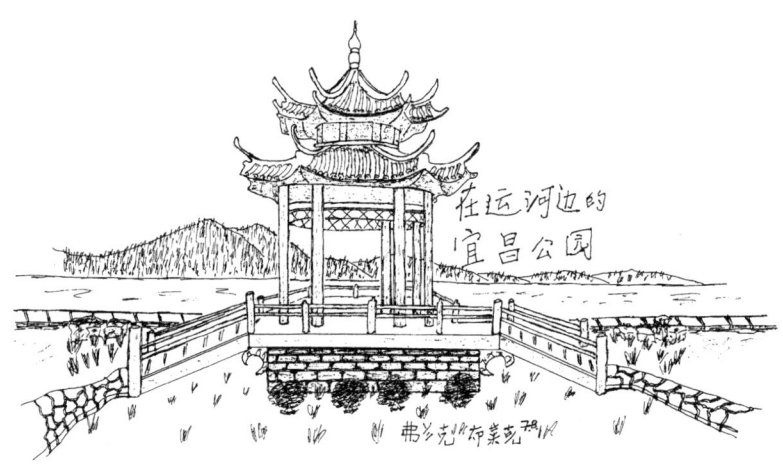

Yichang Park on the Canal

II

An Intimate Look at Chinese Students

> At fifteen I set my heart upon learning.
> - *Confucius*

The responsibility of the Chinese student is described by Pan Qinqin, a Chinese English teacher, this way:

> *I think the job of the students is to try their best to study hard and cooperate with teachers well.*

At the same time, the students have their own opinion of themselves and their responsibility in the classroom. Here's what a forum with seventy-three senior middle school students revealed.

OPEN FORUM WITH SEVENTY-THREE STUDENTS

What time do you get up in the morning?
6:00 a.m. was the specific response by fifty-nine of them while the rest varied between 5:45 a.m. and 6:15 a.m.

What time does your first class start?
At 6:50 a.m., came from all of them and some added that it's a time to hear announcements by the school master. They also said that it is a time to read out loud subject like English, Chinese, and History.

Why do you study so long and so hard?
Eighty percent of the students said that they are studying for money to get a good job. Two students said that they were studying for their parents, while twelve stated that it was their duty.

How is your learning affected by having fifty-nine or more students in the classroom?
Eighteen students admitted that they do their homework carefully and always hand it in because they are deducted marks for not completing either an in-class task or homework assignment. Five students told me that they help each other with homework so that everyone gets along with the teacher. The other 50% said that so many in one classroom cannot compete well; that it is too many students but what can they do?

Do you stand at attention at the beginning of every class?
Yes, we must, came the response from all of them. They also admitted that it is only necessary in Chinese language classes because foreign teachers don't need it.

What time does your last class end?
Our last class ends at 9:50 p.m., after we have finished our homework and study time, was the overall consensus of the group. They admitted it was a long day but added, what can we do?

What do you think about wearing a uniform to school?
Eighty-three percent revealed that they don't like wearing their uniform every day, but added that they must to show the teachers that they are on duty. In some schools, the Monitor wears her school jacket everyday while the Student on Duty sports his jacket only when it's his turn to clean the blackboards, tend to the blackboard

erasers, and sweep the classroom floor. Some of the students commented that they would like the freedom to wear modern clothes and perhaps have their hair a little long or shaved bald.

What is the rule about boyfriends and girlfriends in senior middle school?
One hundred percent of the students that I talked to over the years said that the rule is that we cannot have a boyfriend or a girlfriend because a girlfriend or a boyfriend will take away from studies. Alison, one of the young ladies in senior three, said that a Chinese teacher told her the fastest way to make progress is to make friends with someone who is a different sex. I asked, but she couldn't explain what the statement meant.

Why do you want to learn English?
(1) to get a good job, (2) so I can be rich and travel, (3) to go to abroad.

STUDENT SECRETS REVEALED

The thirty students profiled in the next section, range in age from fourteen to seventeen; the same age as students in grade ten and eleven in Canada. They consider themselves more important than anyone else and want to be surrounded by friends of like-mind. The best students want other best students around them and have low tolerance for the worst students. The worst students also rate themselves more important than anyone else and tend to polarize. The best students have high expectations of one another as revealed in the list below. The best student is sought after eagerly and is not a rarity in a Chinese senior middle school. While it is impossible for one student to have all the attributes that the students have identified bundled into one perfect student, the best academic student, likely the Monitor, chosen by the Chinese Master Teacher, usually has many of the desired characteristics. Here's a collection of words the students used to describe the best student: brave, clever, delightful, easy-going, exciting, friendly, funny, good at sports, hard working, kind, and warm-hearted. And, here's what some of the students wrote about their fellow classmates:

> *I think the best student must be friendly, outgoing, clever, healthy and excited. So I think the best student is He Yi in our class. She is a wonderful girl. She is confident. She is never shy. She studies hard and always helps others. He Yi is our class Monitor.*
>
> *I think Fang Jinshi is the best student in our class because he is clever, proud and also handsome. The important point I think is he always makes me happy, so he is delightful. So, I think he is the best student in our class.*
>
> *Wang Rao is a clever girl. She is our class monitor and is always helpful clever. She likes study. I think she makes efforts very much. She does her homework and reads some books when she has a rest. And she is honest, too. She always makes me happy, so I think she is also a delightful girl.*

When asked to describe a worst student, the formula included impolite, not good at studying, and helpless in that he or she can't find answers to questions without asking everyone around them, hurtful because when one student asked another can I borrow a pen and the answer came back no, the response calculated to worst student. They also said that the worst student is self-absorbed. The worst student is usually avoided by the best student and sometimes even ostracized but rarely neglected.

MOTIVATORS TO LEARN ENGLISH

> *The world is yours, as well as ours, but in the last analysis, it is yours. You young people, full of vigour and vitality, are in the bloom of life, like the sun at eight or nine in the morning. Our hope is placed on you.*
> \- Mao Tse Tung

We came across the courtyard from our last class and there was only one student walking ahead of us carrying an open umbrella. But when we got to the English Corner room, there were twenty-two of them waiting for us, and as many open umbrellas stacked in the corner of the room. My husband and I are foreign experts teaching English as a second language at this senior middle school and are happy to orchestrate the English Corner forums. The students are eager and happy to participate in answering question on what motivates them to learn English as a foreign language. The forum begins with Mu Du, a senior two English study leader.

"Mu Du, do you believe you have a special ability for learning foreign languages?"

"Yes, I do and I also think that I want to learn to speak English very well. I think it's a very useful, helpful and beautiful language from learning it. I can translate it into Chinese when I travel abroad with my parents and friends. So I like it very much and I think I am good at it. I think the best way is participating. Listening, speaking or writing are all necessary, but you must use good and smart methods, if not, everything you've done may be in vain. That's my opinion."

Mu Du smiles as the room fills with applause. Then Zhang Zheng, another senior two student, chooses a question. She reads to the group and then formulates her answer.

"Would you like to have foreign friends? Yes, I'd like to have foreign friends because if I have foreign friends, I will have a good atmosphere to learn English. They can help my English, about speaking, writing, listening, some English grammar and so on. And I will tell them some things about Chinese history. Let them know some things about Chinese history. Let them know more about China. I believe that I will speak English very well with their help. So, if I have chances I hope can make friends with foreigners."

The other group members clap with encouragement for Zhang Zheng who removes her hands from her face to reveal her wide smile. The next speaker, Sun Yun, an English study leader in senior one, gives her opinion about learning English.

"Today, English is so important for all people around the world. If you are not good at English then you can hardly find a job. You can't make much money, too. So, I can't enjoy my life."

Sun Yun passes the bucket filled with questions to her friend and classmate, Song Wei Wei, who dutifully pulls out a slip and reads it to the rest of us.

"Do you want to learn to speak English well? Yes, I do, because English is the most universal language in the world. So, if I can speak English very well, it can help me to found a good job in the future. And I like England very much. If I am good at English, I can get to know England better. So, I must learn to speak English well."

Song Wei Wei reaches over to her friend, Yu Yi, and places a question in her hand. Yu Yi, a senior three student, speaks in a voice that demands attention. It's near perfect North American English pronunciation and accent, is attributed, she says, to watching and mimicking American movies. You can hear her forced capture of the r and the crisp t at the end of some of her words.

"Do you believe that you will learn to speak English very well? First, I like English very much, because I think it sounds well. So, I think and I believe I can learn it very well. More important, English is useful to my life. I can use it to make friends and I can use it to chat with foreign friends so that I can understand other countries' cultures. With this aim, I must learn it well. I learn English by doing listening, reading, writing and speaking. I always watch the English program on the television or on the radio in order to practice my listening. I also read some English newspapers and magazines so that I can speak well and have a nice voice. I'll remember some sentences when I am watching a movie or reading. This can also help my writing so it is necessary and interesting. When I want to relax myself, or when I am in a good mood, I'll read some English. This is the most interesting thing to me. Learning English is a hobby rather than a responsibility to me. I am interested in it, so I believe I can learn it well."

The group explodes with applause while Yu Yi smiles at each of us. Then, Wang Qin Rui, a senior two student, more popularly known to his friends as Johnny, pulls a slip from the container, snaps it twice and reads.

"Do you want to learn English so that you can get to know foreigners better? Let me think. Yes, I do, because we must communicate with the foreigners, so that I can get to know foreign culture better. We can keep the good things for the future reference. We should co-operate with foreigners so I want to learn English so that I get to know foreigners better."

Wang Qin Rui is interrupted by a loud clap of thunder and the knowledge-hungry students scramble to retrieve their packs, jackets and umbrellas. The door is flung open and the students run out. The rain is knocking heavy on the windows and my husband and I are left alone in the room. This session of English Corner is over.

Wang Qin Rui, and students like him at this senior middle school, benefit from the People's Republic of China Compulsory Education law that took effect in 1986 which made requirements and deadlines for the public to receive a free education. The law guaranteed school-age children to the right to receive a nine year education; six years of primary education, and three years of secondary education. However, these public school students' parents still pay several thousand Chinese renminbi, the legal tender in the mainland of People's Republic of China, to have their child attend a school that is designated by the government as *Number 1* school. It's been said that students like Johnny, attending public schools, tend to be more academically successful than those like Mu Du, whose parents are wealthy enough to enrol him in an International Co-operative class without having to make the grade. However, in the case of these English Corner attendees at this round table discussion about what motivates them to learn English as a second language; you've been introduced to some of the most knowledge-hungry students.

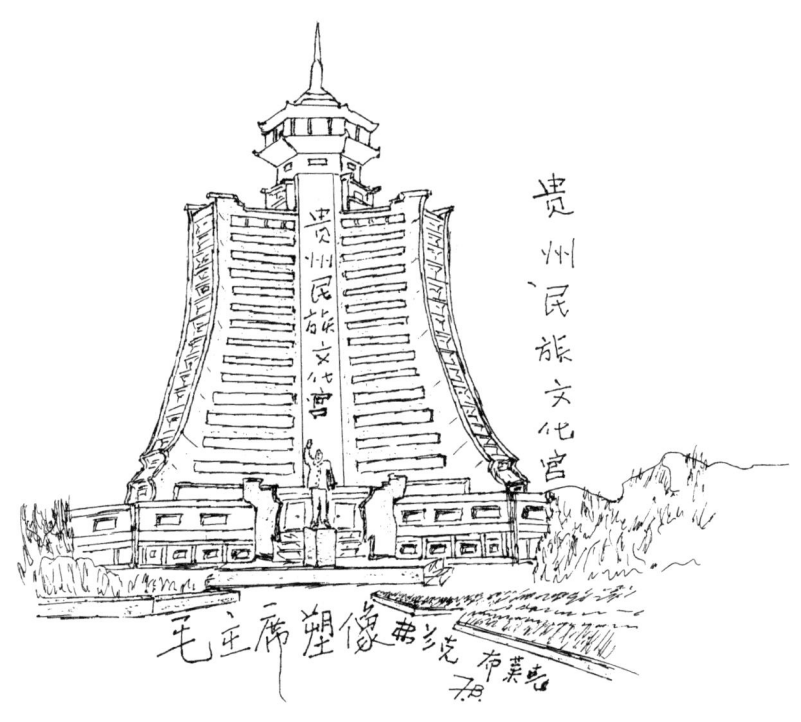

Guiyang Cultural Centre

III

What Chinese Students Believe About Learning English

> Learning without thinking is labour lost; thinking without learning is perilous.
> - *Confucius*

QUESTIONS, ANSWERS AND SIMPLE ANALYSIS

Motivation, defined as *the impetus to create and sustain intentions and goal-seeking acts* (Ames & Ames, 1989), helps the ELS teacher because it determines the extent of the learner's active involvement and attitude toward learning. I became very interested in what determines my student's interest in learning English as a second language quite by accident. While I was rummaging around in the bottom drawer of a desk that once belonged to a teacher who, sadly, didn't make it through his first semester of teaching in China, I found a Horwitz Beliefs about Language

Learning Instrument. It was the questions on the BALLI form that set me in motion to study what motivates my students to learn English as a second language.

The Horwitz Beliefs about Language Learning Instrument is a 34-item Likert-type scale on which respondents mark the degree of agreement and disagreement to each of the thirty-four statements. Questions of enquiry include learner's beliefs about the existence of aptitude, effective learning and communication strategies, the role of age and gender in language learning, the importance of vocabulary, grammar and practice among others. Driven to understand more about the motivation of my students, I located the Banya & Chen 1997 study on the relationships of beliefs about language learning and factors such as motivation. I identified the *instrumental* and *integrative* motivation questions on the BALLI and used those questions, along with a few others related to foreign language aptitude and the nature of language learning, as writing assignments for my students.

Instrumental motivation underlies the goal to gain some social or economical reward through learning a second language and can be considered a functional reason for language learning. *Integrative motivation* is characterized by the learner's positive attitudes towards the target language group and the desire to integrate into the target language community. I received over four hundred and fifty replies from my senior one and two students and selected some for the book. What follows are the 'what you see is what you get' written responses to the questions.

Q: Do you want to learn English very well so that you have better opportunities for a good job?
A1: *Yes, I do. English is widely used in the world. In fact, it has been a second language in China. With a good knowledge of English, I would go abroad to study more and open my eyes, so that I could get a good job and offer my parents a better life. My parents are very important to me. I want*

to make them happy in the rest of their lives. Learning English well is that first step to carry out my plan. Jiang Lu

Jiang Lu is a 17-year-old grade two student and demonstrates *instrumental motivation* by telling us that she wishes to gain social and economic rewards to learning a second language. She has a positive attitude towards language learning and her response reflects a desire and optimism in achieving her language learning goal.

A2: *I believe its right. I will have an opportunity for a good job. I'll have more opportunities to talk with people and use things that I learnt from school. I have never got a job. So I think it will be a good experience and exercise for me.* Wang Zexing

Wang Zexing is 14 years old and in grade one. He also demonstrates instrumental motivation by stating a positive attitude toward learning a second language and is applying a functional reason for learning English.

Q: Do you want to learn to speak English well?

A1: *Yes, I want to learn English very well. Because I hope to have a good job in future. I want to get married with my wife to look after her and my son. I hope we have a good life.* Ji Ke

Ji Ke is 16 years old and shows instrumental motivation tendency with his hopes for a good job in the future. He makes clear his need for social and economic rewards.

A2: *I want to do. Because I like English. At first I read English words and write a lot of subject, carry lots of words before me.* Chen Cheng

Chen Cheng is a 17-year-old grade one student and appears to be motivated by his like for the English language. Motivation is defined as the learner's orientation with regard to the goal of learning a second language.

A3: *After senior examination I chose Guiyang Number One High School. The reason why I chose here is just because you Mrs. Black and all the for-*

eign teachers. Yes I love English. I have been thinking of going abroad since I was in middle school. Foreign countries attract me a lot. Canada is the place where I want to go most. Once I watched a TV program called 'Small International Students' it told a story about four Chinese students who studied in Canada. I was deeply touched by it. From then on I decided to study English well and go abroad when graduated. So I never think studying English is a task but rather a skill. And I have strong confidence that I will learn English well. Believe me, I will one day make my dream come true. David

David, whose Chinese name is Mao Kai Jie, is a 15-year-old grade one student with ambitions of learning English very well and also a love for the English language. David demonstrates instrumental motivation because his intention is to gain social and economical reward through learning English as a second language.

Q: Do you believe that you will learn to speak English very well?
A1: I think I can learn to speak English very well because I like English and I think it's easier to learn English than Chinese. My teacher told me if we wanted to learn a language well, we should learn hearing, speaking, reading and writing well. So I think I will spend some free time watching English movie, that is very interesting and it can improve my hearing. Second I will read some books which I am interested in. Oh, I have a good idea to practice my writing that is use English to write daily what about speaking? I think I can speaking English with my friends maybe it's a good way. Cinderella

Cinderella, whose Chinese name is Li Jiao Yang, is a 16-year-old grade one student. She reveals her many methods of learning the language and seems genuinely interested and motivated to continue. She likes English and that is what is instrumentally motivating her.

A2: I do. I like English very well. Firstly, I believe I have enough confidence to do it well. Secondly, I will make some talk to you. I'll also watch some English speaking movie of series such as Prison Break. Listen carefully to conversation and comprehend it then repeat it. In all, I'll do it by anyway I can. Chooco

I get a kick out of Chooco's determination to make English his second language. Chooco, whose Chinese name is Sun Li, is a 15-year-old grade one student and is a Computer Leader. His like for English is instrumental in improving his English.

Q: Do you want to learn English so that you can get to know foreigners better?
A: *Yes, I do. Because I want to go to another country. I like many countries. Such as England, Canada and so on. I want to know foreign culture and make friends with foreigners. So I want to study English well now.* Fish

Fish's Chinese name is Wen Jing, and he's 16 years old. His motivation to learn English is positive and *integrative* because he wants to integrate into the target language community.

Q: Is learning a foreign language different than learning other school subjects?
A: *As far as I am concerned, I do believe that we can't say that whether learning a foreign language is different than learning other school subjects or not. But I couldn't but to say that there's some connections between them. Just take the Chinese for example; English also need to recite many things. Obviously, accumulation is the most effective way in learning both of the language. In other side, English isn't our mother tongue, we cannot use it freely like the way we use Chinese. From this we have not hard to draw a conclusion that learning a foreign depend on you attitude towards it. If you really like it from your deep heart, it will be the most subject, if not, the result turns out bad. Further more, we need to comprehend every learning points, how are learning a foreign language is quite different. What we need is a process of accumulation. Over what had been mentioned above, we can't say different or same absolutely.* Vanny

Vanny, known to her Chinese friends as Xiao Yun Fang Yu, is a 17-

year-old grade two student. She addresses the nature of language learning in a very eloquent way. She realizes that there is some connections between them but isn't ready to say that learning a foreign language is different than learning another school subject. Vanny also points out that motivation in learning English has to do with the learner's attitude towards it.

Q: Do you believe that people in China feel it is important to speak English?
A: *First of all, I think English is an international language. Therefore, it is necessary for us to learn it. So, in my opinion, people in China feel it is really important for everyone to speak English. If we can speak English well, we can communicate with Englishmen to know something about their custom or history. Also we can read something in English for fun. For example, from the Internet we can enjoy it. Second, if you speak English well, we can travel to a lot of English-speaking countries to meet lots of friends. It's so great. In this way, we also make friends with others from all over the world. So, I agree with this idea in the question.* Yang Jie Xin

Yang Jie Xin is a 15-year-old grade one student. Her opinion demonstrates instrumental motivation because she tells her functional reason for learning English.

Q: Do you believe that the most important part of learning a foreign language is learning the grammar?
A1: *No, I don't because I think the most important part of learning a foreign language is that you enjoy it and will be happy when you learn it. So I think you will learn the foreign language well.* Zhang Ming Yang

Zhang Ming Yang, an 18-year-old grade two student, tells us that learning grammar makes her unhappy. Her opinion represents a student's actual language learning practice and it looks as though Zhang Ming Yang is ready to embrace a lesser focus on form and rule learning, such as Communicative Language Teaching offers.

A2: *Grammar isn't the most important thing when learning English. In my opinion, the aim of education is action, but not examination. Perhaps, for worst students, learning grammar is just for exam. So they don't care about speaking at all. I think the aim of learning English is speaking. If one can only do exercise but can't talk with others, we can say he doesn't learn the main spirit of English. So I think if one studies grammar simply, he can't learn English well. We students ought to read more original articles and listen to the tape and read loudly. The more we read the better we will learn English.* Ke Jin Du

Ke Jin Du is a 16-year-old grade one student ahead of his time in China in regards to learning English grammar. In his careful speech about the nature of language learning, he expresses his belief in the spirit of a language and suggests a shift in student-preferred learning methodologies.

Q: Do you believe that people who speak more than one language are very intelligent?

A1:   *I agree. Because I think language is important in our lives. If you speak more than one language then the boss will know you are better! Language can train my brain. It can make us more clever.* Zhang Yu

Zhang Yu is an 18-year-old grade two student and expresses his thoughts on foreign language aptitude by suggesting that his personal intelligent quotient affects his acquiring additional languages.

A2:   *I think so, because we can talk about it with different people and can get more knowledgeable.* Long Feng Hai

Long Feng Hai, also an 18-year-old grade two student, believes that knowing another language makes you more knowledgeable, which can be interpreted as intelligence.

The sweet wisdom provided by the students in the above answers help identify the student's instrumental and integrative motivations for learning English as a second other language. Along with providing direct answers to direct questions, some of the students wrote notes to me. Here are a few of them:

> *The world needs English. Learning English is my hobby. English is my favourite subject. I go for English without reason. Although sometime I feel bored and tired, I still devote myself to it.* Zhang Hau Yang

> *After I took part in English Corner this term, I felt very happy and lucky. I improve my oral English. Second and it's the most important point that I made a lot of friends there. We open our ears open our eyes open our heart to communicate with each other. Give our opinion over some serious topic.* Millie

> *At the beginning, English was a little difficult for me, especially the vocabulary part. After I've learned 1,000 words, it became easier. But then I spoke to the foreigners I found that the words I could understand in a passage and the words I could write just couldn't jump out of my mouth. I know that the spoken English also need practice. Language is communication. Now I'm trying. It's really a hard but a happy job.* Liu Zhi Yu

> *First I want to say I'm interested I English very much. I want to go abroad for education to communicate with western culture. In my opinion I think learning English need a kind of gift, talent. But if you're interested in it you'll put you heart into it and then you'll be a good English speaker. A lot of people think they're not interested in it but I think a hobby is come from the developing of ability. You can be interested in everything if you try!* Li Ni Yi

On a pedagogical level, the above questions, answers and simple analysis along with the students' comments about learning English, support the fundamental arguments raised by many academic researchers that understanding learners' beliefs can enhance the language learning process. Wenden (1986) suggested that classroom activities in which learners examine and evaluate their own beliefs may lead to increased awareness and modification of their expectations concerning language learning. Additionally, Horwitz (1987) reported on teachers' testimonies of how discussions at the beginning of an English as a second language course related to their beliefs and expectations helped to clear up some of their students' misconceptions about language learning, which Horwitz notes – are often based on limited experience and knowledge. Therefore, it is reasonable to conclude that TESOL teachers' consciousness of learners' beliefs and expectations "may contribute to a more conducive learning environment and to more effective learning" (Chawhan & Oliver, 2000:25).

> *A single conversation with a wise man is better than ten years of study.*
> *- Chinese Proverb*

Caption: Great Wall of China

IV

The International Co-operative Class

> ...education cannot alter the inner essence of a man, but it doth exert tremendous influence, and with this power it can bring forth from the individual whatever perfections and capacities are deposited within him.
> - Adu'l-Baha

When you're looking for a teaching job in China, you are likely to come across many job advertisements from public schools and private schools and from schools that are a combination of both. The schools that provide both public and private instruction refer to the public students as public and the private's students as International Co-operative students. There are distinct differences between the two; monetarily and academically, which have huge implications on the student's motivation for learning any subject including English as a second language. A foreign teacher who has an understanding of these differences will be best prepared for the challenge of teaching English as a second language in China.

China's economic expansion has lead to an increase in demand for education at all levels, and the establishment of private kindergartens, middle schools and high schools, colleges and universities is encouraged by the government. These institutions charge relatively high fees and claim to offer better facilities and equipment, smaller classes and better teachers. One of the biggest marketing strategies for this type of school is to emphasize the size and quality of its teaching staff.

Unfortunately, these claims are not always backed up by reality. As in any sector, high demand combined with inadequate regulation causes low quality service provision. Private schools are often seen as options only for rich families whose children do not have the academic ability to get into the grade-demanding public schools. It's common knowledge among Chinese teachers who are strapped with the International Co-operative students that high concentrations of them have failed elsewhere, and that these classes are much more driven by profit than education.

The establishment of an International Co-operative class is a unique and convoluted alliance between a foreign education institution, the Chinese government and a school. For example, a foreign university pays the Chinese government a mysterious amount of money to have an English program at one of its schools with the hopes that the graduates will head off to their university. The high school uses some of the foreign money to hire foreign experts to teach English as a second language. The wealthy Chinese parents pay the school even more money to enrol their child or children in the English language program, and according to one Chinese English teacher at a high school in Guiyang province, it gets worse.

Here's what Yu Fang, a young Chinese English teacher says about her International Co-operative students.

> *Here's what I can say about the International Co-operative class students in this building. Classes from 25 to number 32 are very different in this school. The students pay more money*

than the other students, because their marks to entering high school are lower. They have special lessons, for example they have more lessons with foreign teachers than others. Most of students in this building are of parents of much money. They needn't worry about their future. All of them don't need to go to university. To find a good job in the future is not the main aim for them.

Last week I gave up on some of the students in Class 27. That's the truth. I don't think I need to waste a lot of time trying to encouraging them to study. It is unnecessary. I began to teach the students of number 27 last June. I feel I have a very bad mood when I try to be with them. It is very hard to express my feelings. As a teacher I think it is my responsibility to encourage my students to study well, but I feel that when I face the students in 27, some of them are not listening to what I said. So, I can only be responsible for the students who want to study. But the students don't talk a lot in my class. I needn't be very angry with them. So, I let them be. If they want to read novels, I let them be, I don't care. The students in my class don't listen. If they are reading, I leave them be. The students in this building are just an exhibition. They are quite different from the other students.

Sometimes I think it is hopeless. Because I think as a teacher, there is a conflict. As a teacher it is my responsibility to let all the students study to get better at English. But in this case of the International Co-operative students,, I don't think it is a good idea; but I cannot let them bother the good students. For me the most important thing is that we let them follow the good students. Because most of the students want to study, they are eager to study. But the technique of letting the bad students do what they want to do is against me. How about the other students? How to get them to listen? What are they doing? How will they get better at English? I must improve their four abilities in English or I will not graduate with the students, I will be left in grade two. These students must pass a final examination. But your examination, your score will not be added up to their total score. So, I don't teach the students in the same way as you. In other words, my teaching is continuous; they need to listen to me in every class. But they don't listen and we cannot make them listen. We cannot speak to the students' parents because it is no use.

Here is a story that the Head Master of the school told me. He said one day after the meeting held for all the parents, the Head Teacher had a talk with one of the parents. He said your son has done something bad recently. You should try to persuade him to listen to the teacher to study well to study something useful in school. What did the parent say? He said let him be. I don't care. I am a boss. There are many undergraduates in my company. I don't think they are the best. I don't think the only way to get a job is to enter a university. I don't think education is the most important thing for my son. I only want him to stay here to keep safe.

So, sometimes talking to parents is not the useful way. Most students in this building are very special. They are from a rich family. If they cannot pass the grade, their parents can pay for them to study abroad. If you have money all things can be done.

You talked about putting them into groups. I did try this but it did not work because they could not talk. For example, I ask them about water and water formation from Unit 12, and I ask them about what you can do with water, play, wash, drink. But they cannot talk about it because they don't understand about water in English. One of the problems is that they cannot express themselves in their writing. But they can be improved.

Another problem is that when only about two-thirds hand in their work. I can only improve the students who want to study. For the other students, I can do nothing.

Another problem is that you cannot punish the students in this special class. Our Head Master said you cannot punish the students. If there is something wrong with the students and you ask them to get out, the Monitor will tell the Head Master and the teacher will be in trouble. Even if I keep a *name of the student and show it to the parent, some of the parents don't give a care.*

All I can do is encourage the students that want my help and reward them with my help. I encourage all my students. But even if I do these things, there are students that still ignore you. If I get angry with them, I waste some time. I don't want to waste time dealing with bad students. I feel sad though that the rights of the International Co-operative students are upper class. In this school we are the opposite, we teachers belong to the lowest class.

In the case of this high school in Guiyang, it was ordered by school administration that the foreign expert English teachers give the students reading, writing, listening and speaking examinations at the end of each semester. However, much to our surprise, several of the Chinese colleagues told us that the marks collected from the foreign teachers were not added or blended into the marks given by the Chinese English teachers.

PRISONERS OF THE INTERNATIONAL CO-OPERATIVE CLASS

September 4, 2006, a day that will forever be etched in my memory, I stand in a classroom in China. In the heat of the afternoon the classroom holds two young girls who sit cosy on a small stool, their cheeks pressed close to share a set of music-player earphones. The girls are oblivious to the young boy slouched at his desk reading a Chinese textbook, and the young man bouncing a basketball, the hollow thud echoing off the brick walls. According to the student attendance roster I hold, these International Co-operative students will eventually number fifty-nine. By the end of today's first forty-minutes, I will decide that this gathering of students is not a normal class, and, by the end of the week, I will secretly refer to these students as prisoners, a label borrowed from a professor at teacher's college who said that anyone who doesn't want to be where you are is a prisoner. My biggest challenge for this large crowd was to prepare a lesson plan that would engage all the students long enough so that the keeners wouldn't lose their motivation and the prisoners would attach an intrinsic value to learning English.

I put on easy listening music in the hopes that the students will like it and attach value to the song they hear, and soon three other students arrive, and then a group of five saunters in. I count seventeen students that stream through the door and then calculate that thirty are still missing. I stand at the doorway and usher in the six students loitering in the hall. Three young girls sweep past me and then a swarm of students rush in pushing and shoving each other until they settle on their stools. The bell chimes to announce the start of our English as a second language class. I turn off the easy-listening music and announce the interviewing task to be performed this day. I see five students looking up at me, twelve students talking and five who have their heads on their arms, three students fanning themselves with paper fans, and two tossing a basketball back and forth. I stop tracking them and continue with my teaching duty. What I reveal next is a few of the questions I asked these students at the beginning of the school year to help me identify my audience. Here are a few of the conversations I had with the students:

> "How old are you?"
> "Sixteen," says Shi Yang Tao Tao.
> "How long have you been studying English?"
> "Four, mmm, four years."
> "Why do you want to learn English?"
> "I want to know, uh, foreigners because, uh, mmm, because I want to go, mmm, uh, Canada, future. So, I want to know foreigners better."
> "How old are you?"
> "Sixteen," says Chen Cheng.
> "How long have you been studying English?"

"Six, six."
"Do you think that it is important to speak English?"
"No, I don't think so."
"Can you tell me why?"
"Because I don't have to speak it."
"How old are you?"
"Fifteen," says Zhou Run Zu.
"Do you want to study English?"
"I have no choice."
"If you had a choice, would you want to study English?"
"In the beginning I study but now I don't want to."

These few samples of one-on-one interviews are evidence of the forty-six of the fifty-nine students who weren't interested in learning English as a second language in this International Co-operative class. In contrast, thirteen students told me of their various beliefs about learning English as a second language including a desire to get to know foreigners better, a better opportunity for a good job, and some of them told me that they each had a special ability to learn a foreign language. The notable difference between these preliminary interviews and the ones that I held at the end of the year was that there was no notable difference at all. The 'don't want to learn English' bunch of students only reduced to thirty-seven. The students in this particular International Co-operative class are from some of the wealthiest families in China and are comparable in age to grade eleven students in Canada. The majority of them do not want to be here, a fact quantified when I asked each student the question do you want to learn English? Their response was no.

"Please don't be offended," says Ye Jiao, my student interpreter, in a private conversation with me. "Most of the students don't understand you. They can't speak English and don't understand what you say."

Cop out? My mind sings with the opinion of a fellow foreign expert, Glenn Lion, who has been teaching at this school for three years.

"The students complain to the head teacher that they don't understand you because they are so far behind in their English language study that they are ashamed of their inability with the language. It's a cop out! They've been studying English for at least six years, but there's no one to talk to and so they loose it. Use it or loose it, right?" Glenn concludes.

On Sunday, June 23, 2007, I finish the last of the year-end student interviews and conclude that although some of the three hundred and fifty-four students in my six International Co-operative classes could still be identified as prisoners, at least one hundred and six of them had improved their English capabilities. At the beginning of the year, battles took place between me and a few of the students in my International Co-operate classes, and then conversations took place between us. The early battles dissolved into friendly communication and that communication grew into consultation and now, at end of the year, I have changed my mind about them and it's filled with fondness.

> *Our attitude towards ourselves should be 'to be satiable in learning' and towards others 'to be tireless in teaching'.*
> *- Mao Tse Tung*

Pudong Park

V

For Your Information

> One must spend time in gathering
> knowledge to give it out richly.
> - Edward C. Steadman

A BREAKTHROUGH IN CULTURE SHOCK

The Collins-Cobuild Advanced Learner's English Dictionary says that culture consists of activities such as the arts and philosophy, which are considered to be important for the development of civilization and of people's minds. A culture is a particular society or civilization, especially considered in relation to its beliefs, way of life, or art. The culture of a particular organization or group consists of the habits of the people in it and the way they generally behave. In science, a culture is a group of bacteria or cells which are grown, usually in a laboratory as part of an experiment. It's when that experiment goes horribly wrong that people experience their first stage of *culture shock*.

Culture shock is a feeling of anxiety, loneliness, and confusion that people sometimes experience when they first arrive in a country very different from their own. Take your time with those feelings and their comings and goings. Recognize those different feelings, your culture shock feelings, but try not to fight them, let them be and let them become who you are. According to Schumann's Theory of Acculturation, you will move through the following culture shock stages: 1. The Euphoric Stage, 2. The Hostile Stage, 3. The Acceptance Stage, 4. The Reverse Culture Shock Stage. It's the *Acceptance Stage* that you can look forward to having the most fun with, a laughing out loud, holding your gut kind of fun. It's in stage three of culture shock that you will learn to accept the differences between your host country and your home country and you'll celebrate, in your own way, those differences where appropriate. There are certain customs that the host country reserves that will become part of your everyday life. A good example might be pushing your way onto a bus in China, ignoring any memory or duty to queuing. You know you've been in China long enough when that happens. Here's a sampling of a few *you know you've been in China long enough when...*

- you feel an overwhelming sense of safety
- you eat noodles for breakfast
- you can hum Chinese songs
- you're able to order more than noodles
- you walk where there's less car traffic - on the sidewalk
- you're OK wearing your winter coat while eating indoors
- frog tastes like chicken
- you don't hear yourself slurping
- you don't gag at the spitting
- you carry toilet paper everywhere
- you can give the taxi driver your home address in Chinese

BANKING AT THE BANK OF CHINA

The Bank of China is located in cities all over China. To open a bank account as a foreign expert, we recommend you deal with the main branch because they may have one person who can speak a few words of English. To open an account at the Bank of China, you'll need your passport, your foreign expert certificate, a letter of employment from your employer, and ten to one hundred renminbi. The ten RMB is needed to open your account and it will be returned to you when you physically return to the same branch to withdraw all your money and close your account.

Exchanging currency from RMB to American dollars can be a convoluted process if you choose to go into the bank because you will have to present bank management with a list of duties you perform at your workplace, your foreign expert certificate, tax information, your work visa and passport. It can take anywhere from one hour to three, to process your request depending on the bank's experience with performing foreign money exchange. Or, you can take your bundle of RMB and have the *money-changer* do it. You will recognize the money-changer as the person who stands just outside the bank property holding a bulging bag.

FOUR ESSENTIALS FOR CHINA POST

China Post is focusing on the corporate culture build up, uplifting the workforce quality by sharpening its' employees skills and by providing continued training. Well, that's great but you need training before attempting to mail something out of China. First, you'll need a black-ink ball point pen to write the return address. Second, you'll need to purchase an envelope that has the distinct Air Mail sticker on it because if you've already addressed your envelope and it doesn't have the sticker on it, they will kindly glue the marked envelope on top of yours and then instruct you to readdress your envelope with the black-ink ball point pen. It doesn't occur to the China Post employee to cut the Air Mail stamp from the new envelope and simply glue it to your addressed envelope because that act is not permissible. Thirdly, you are required to only partially pack anything that you're sending home, leaving the contents exposed at one end to share your package contents with a China Post employee, who you can't speak to anyway, but more to be sure that the Chinese characters are readable so that the employee can determine if your package is safe to ship. Fourthly, if you're sending anything by China Post EMS (Express Mail Service), be aware that its service ends in Hong Kong because Hong Kong is considered a foreign country by Beijing and the tracking system ends at the Hong Kong border. You only find out that EMS switches to TNT, another courier service, when your Chinese friend calls the China Post EMS Chinese-only helpline on your behalf. EMS is known for it's inside China expedient service. In our case, the package was sent December 19 and was picked up in Vancouver, Canada, on January 2. Our Chinese friend said it was held in Hong Kong for a while because it came to their attention that there was a holiday in Canada.

WHAT IS A NUMBER ONE SCHOOL?

For your information, I've taught at four schools in China so far that are combined with public classes and private or international co-operative classes and three of them have been identified as No.1 Junior Middle School or No.1 Senior Middle School. Here's what Li Ying, a Chinese English teacher said about how a school in China gets assigned the number one designation.

> The government put several schools together to form a new one and named it number one around the liberation. And other new schools founded later were named number two, three, four, and so on. Since number one has the longest history and the most teaching experience, it is usually the best one in almost every city in China.

HOW TO BE A READY, WILLING AND ABLE FOREIGN TEACHER

> *The thing about anything in life is you have to get ready for it. Study, learn and in terms of teaching, there's a lot to learn. The bigger culture you have in life, the better teacher you'll be.*
>
> - adapted from Jacqueline Bisset
> - Interview on "Chats from the Past"

My husband and sometime teaching partner, discovered very quickly after stepping into our first classroom in China, that although we were willing and capable of teaching English, we didn't necessarily know what time of day the students had their first class or what was accomplished in that first class. We didn't know why they were studying for such long hours or how their learning was affected by fifty-nine or more students in one classroom. We didn't know why they stood at attention in Chinese-teacher-led classes and not in ours, or how they felt about wearing a uniform to school or the historical rule about boyfriend and girlfriend relationships, or when the last class of the day ended. You can be a ready, willing and able foreign teacher in China, by asking your students questions about their learning culture.

Qidong Canal

VI

Confessions from China

> *It's not hard to find the truth. What is hard is not to run away from it once you have found it.*
> *- unknown*

THE MIDNIGHT RUNNER

The midnight runner is a mysterious foreign teacher who makes an escape from China. The midnight runner can't tolerate the bulky bureaucracy of the Chinese school system or the personalities of the students who attend his classes, or his work colleagues; or simply, he is not ready, willing or able to adapt to teaching in China. The midnight runner tries to make sense of the Chinese culture and constantly compares China to his home country but can't see the similarities only the differences and hates them. The midnight runner can't force people to change and realizes that he can't wait for them to change and doesn't have the patience for them any longer. There have been hundreds of midnight runners who have made an escape from China and each runner has his or her own reason for leaving. Take Bob for instance, an English teacher who spent two school semesters in China and by the middle of the first semester of his second year, successfully committed a midnight run.

In the 1988 version of the movie called *The Midnight Run*, it's an accountant who is chased by bounty hunters, the American Federal Bureau of Investigation, and the Mafia after jumping bail. In this 2007 version of what felt like a comedy movie to me but a drama movie for Bob, it's an English teacher who is being chased by his personal ghosts, faceless conscience and his Chinese girlfriend.

Bob and his girlfriend lived in a furnished apartment on school campus, received free two eighteen litre canisters of bottled water once a week, free international and local telephone service, free internet connection, free once-a-month van transport to WalMart, wrote the odd scratchy lesson plan, listened to music and had free built-in Mandarin lessons, yet, Bob was not happy.

"Well, that's it!" Bob shouts as he stomps past me into the apartment. He finds the empty chair and flops down, crossing his legs and folding his arms in one motion. He's sitting across from my husband and says to him, "How can you stand it here? They drive me crazy. The kids drive me crazy and the stupid administration drives me crazy. They just ignore me. Crap!" Bob's waving his arms over his head as he continues. "Xie Wei called me today and told me that I can't have Ming in the apartment anymore I'm pissed at Xie Wei and her Chinese judgemental flack." Bob stops, looks up at me and murmurs, "I think it's time I made my escape."

Xie Wei is the Director of the Foreign Services Department at this school in China, a strong woman whose job it is to enforce the rules for teacher conduct. Bob met with her two days before the 'get the girlfriend out' phone call to defend his conduct in class. He'd been reported on by the class Monitor who dutifully told her Head Teacher that Bob had called his students stupid. This incident was then reported by the Head Teacher to Xie Wei.

"We received a complaint from the students that you called them stupid."

"Yah, well it didn't happen that way."

"What way did it happen? Can you tell me please?"

"I told the kids that their behaviour in class was stupid and that acting stupid makes them stupid."

"Bob, we would like you to apologize to the students. Would you do that please?"

"Apologize? I think they should apologize to me for acting out in class and not paying attention and listening to music in my class and talking Chinese in my class! How about that?"

"It is not acceptable in any culture to call someone stupid, so please tell the class you are sorry. Would you do that please?"

Bob lifts himself from his chair and puts on a smile. "Sure," he says, and walks away from Xie Wei leaving her, the cold room and their verbal agreement behind.

I listen as Bob continues, "I'm tired of the disrespect I get from the school and the students. Well, OK, some of the kids are great but the co-op classes are rude and disrespectful and I didn't come all this way to be bashed around by the Chinese."

Bob is referring to the students in the foreign-funded English international co-operative classes we teach that are filled with over-the-top rich kids who don't have to be in school weren't it for their parents wanting a place for them to be when they are at work.

Bob opens his mouth wide and spills a loud laugh. "Do you remember the time Drew tried to have an interview with Xie Wei and she kept answering her phones? Remember how Drew got nutty because Wei paid more attention to her phones than him and he threw both cells and they smashed against the wall?" Bob calms his face and jaw and continues, his face dissolving into concern. "Drew made his midnight run after that and I don't want it to get like that for me."

My husband and I left for holidays that night and when we returned this note was under our door. *Hi, by the time you read this I will be long gone. I left my apartment unlocked, help yourself to the stuff I left behind. Just tell people you don't know anything, you came back and I was gone. Bye and hope you have a good term.* Bob

With the disappearance of Bob, it seemed a practical solution to my husband who is also a TESOL teacher and who was available at no extra cost because he was right there in the school quarters, that I suggest to Xie Wei that he take over Bob's teaching duties so that the students wouldn't suffer the consequence of him leaving. But, for some reason unknown to us, my husband wasn't hired. Instead, an American fellow who claimed to have his Masters in Mental Health Services was flown in to teach the students. He didn't last his first month. His biggest complaint to me was that there is no personal space available to foreigners whether they are shopping, hiking, taking a ride on the bus or running.

"Even running away isn't enough of a clue for them," Dan told me once, his face scrunched up in anger.

Dan became the third midnight runner at our school that term.

THE CONSEQUENCE OF TRUTH

If you knew that your truth would cause a devastating consequence, would you change your truth? Let me talk to you about the truth and consequence of one of my lesson plans delivered at a senior middle school in China. The lesson plan consisted of statements that I would read to the students and they were to decide if the sentence was fact or opinion. The truthful statement that caused the shocking consequence was: CHINA IS BEAUTIFUL. This pleasant little sentence was used as a spark to ignite the reporting on me by the classroom Monitor to the Vice Principal of the school. I read the statement to the students and they shouted yes, which I then wrote in the opinion column on the blackboard.

"It's a fact not an opinion," says Wu Jun Kun from the front row.

I recognize his voice and turn to look at him. Wu Jun Kun is the

English Study Leader in this international co-operative class and has developed a strong confidence in responding to English language prompts.

"Thank you for your opinion, Wu Jun Kun," I say and then speak to the class, "my opinion is that it is not a fact."

"You're wrong! Then, Canada is not beautiful!" one student shouts.

I look for the source of the voice but cannot locate it.

"That again is your opinion," I say to the class.

That was our final exchange; I had a mutiny on my hands after that. None of the students would respond to any more of the fact or opinion statements and later that day, I was called into the Vice-Principal's office. Her Chinese name is Ye Er Pu, but she's invited the foreign English teachers to call her Shelly. Shelly invites me to sit down on a thick leather chair in her office and proceeds to tell me that a student from Class 26, Grade 2, reported to her that I was speaking badly about China. She tells me not to speak about China in any of my classrooms any more. I try to tell my side of the story but she puts her hand up to stop me. I acknowledge her body language with my own action of a nod and then lift myself from the chair and leave her office. That afternoon, I receive an email from my recruiter in Canada and part of the message reads:

> *You need to be more culturally sensitive. It is important to get in touch with the reasons you went to China in the first place, to live, to learn, to explore, to teach English and gain a greater understanding about another culture.*

That evening I receive a phone call from the Chinese employment placement company, the company who deposits my salary into my bank account, and he suggests that I take the Vice-Principal's advice and not speak of China in my classroom. I had no idea that such a truth could cause such a consequence. I haven't used the lesson plan since.

COMMUNISM IN THE CLASSROOM

I never thought that I'd love communism in my classroom as much as I would hate the mimicked thunderous sound of a fast moving train. The sound is deafening as I walk toward a classroom that contains strange students in a strange school in a strange country strangled by a strange culture. I step closer to the doorway and then stop in its frame. The thunder stops and fifty-nine pairs of teenage eyes stare into mine. I hear one voice shout two syllables in a language I don't understand and it scatters the students in all directions to their desks where they sit and in near perfect unison fold their hands in front of them. One student remains standing at the back of the classroom, his arms straight beside his body, his eyes front. I step through the doorway and up onto the platform at the top of the classroom and face the students. I place my school bag on the desk and turn to face the blackboard. I write my name in large letters and turn around.

"Good morning students."

A thunder clap fills the room and at the same time the students stand at attention and chant in unison, "good morning teacher."

Oh, how wonderful and I smile my widest to express my thrill and say, "my name is Mrs. Black and I am from Canada. I am here to help you improve your English. I am happy to meet all of you. Have a seat, please."

The students react with soldier-like precision, sit, backs straight, on their wooden stools. The student at the back remains standing, arms close to his body, back straight, eyes front.

"What is your name?"

"Qiu Fang Xu."

"Qiu Fang Xu," I say, and the room explodes with laughter at my pronunciation.

Qiu Fang Xu barks a command and the class falls silent. He says, "may I take my seat?"

"Of course."

The final thirty-four minutes of the class is maintained with combinations of orders snapped by the Monitor and an exchange of glances between him and me. It is absolutely delicious. I love that the Monitor's duty is dictated by the communist style of dedication to duty and that his primary duty is to help me maintain order in the classroom. Ah, but alas, it doesn't last long because before the week was out the students realized that this foreigner's approach to classroom behaviour, although strongly driven by respect, also encourages open communication and conversation.

PLEASE FORGIVE THEM, FOR THEY KNOW NOT WHAT THEY DO

3:56 p.m. Beijing Time
In the Middle of a Sit-In Protest

It is three fifty-six in the afternoon and Daisy is holding a one person sit-in at the front of her classroom in a high school in China. The air in November is white as it spills from her mouth and floats in front of her face. She adjusts her red wool scarf with her gloved hands.

"Please, Daisy, you must forgive them for sometimes they don't know what they do," Wang Zhu says pleadingly. "Please come with me to Zhang Yu Ping's office and we talk there."

The young woman standing over Daisy is the Foreign Affairs Director's assistant, and the Foreign Affairs Director, Zhang Yu Ping, is the person who, Daisy believes, can help squelch the class discipline problems that plague her and the three foreign experts and twice as many Chinese English teachers at this Number One Senior Middle School in China. Daisy looks up at Wang Zhu and meets her gaze. She sees calm in Wang Zhu's face and a wide, bright smile. Daisy looks down at the concrete floor trying desperately to push back her pent up anger over the months of student abuse, but it bulges and pulses in her head as she looks up again at Wang Zhu. Daisy hears other words come from the young woman, "we don't speak of student matters in front of the class. We speak in private and then speak to the student privately. It's the Chinese way."

The storm troopers in Daisy's head prepare to blast their way past her tongue into the frosty air. She forces her lips together and represses the harsh words she intends to shout at Wang Zhu and all the students. It's a sit-in protest her thoughts tell her. For once in your life hold on to what you believe in and what you want. Daisy obeys and remains seated on the cold platform at the front of the classroom. Before this day is over Daisy will be offered a week's reprieve from the discipline problems that defy her abilities at classroom management but sadly will leave a mark that restricts her being invited back to teach a second semester.

3:30 p.m. Beijing Time
The Build Up to a Sit-In Protest

At three-thirty in the afternoon, Daisy walks the familiar fifteen steps of her classroom to reach the last two desks whose occupants are cheek to cheek viewing the contents of a Chinese glossy magazine. Daisy stands close to the students noting that the stack of textbooks on their desks does not have the required English textbook among them.

"What class is this?"

Wang Yimeng slowly turns her expressionless face up at Daisy and blinks. Daisy's mind counts one-thousand, two-thousand, three-thousand, four-thousand, five-thousand, and then repeats the question.

"English".

"Yes, this is English class. OK, then which book should be on your desk?"

The black-haired student slams shut the Chinese magazine and tosses it into her desk shelf.

"Thank you. Now if you could please open your English textbook to page thirty-three, we can get started," Daisy says, straining a smile, and then turns to another student, asks the same question and performs the same ritual. The first three conversations are successful; the fourth student isn't budging.

"What class is this, Wang Chi?"

Wang Chi stares back at her but continues to flip through his Chinese workbook.

"What class is this?" Daisy asks, but the Chinese youth doesn't answer and Daisy's mind drifts back to the advice she received from her friend, Janice, a fourteen-year veteran at a high school in Canada, "don't engage in a power struggle with the kids because you'll always lose." Daisy stands quietly and looks around the room at the sea of students. I'm here because I love teaching she tells herself as she walks away from the Chinese youth. She ignores the loud voices drowning out her own and continues with the explanation of the lesson plan but within a few minutes she can no longer resist the temptation gnawing at her control ego and singles out a Chinese boy who she believes defies her. Daisy walks to the student and stands beside him to interrupt his conversation. Two things happen – first Janice's advice turns into mush and second the youth continues to talk to his desk mate in rapid Chinese.

"Do you have a question for me, Jacky?"

"Do you have a question for me?" he mimics and adds, "no."

"OK, then, please don't talk while I'm talking."

Immediately the Chinese youth resumes talking and Daisy turns to face him, her reference to all classroom management techniques dissipate into the thin cold air. Daisy's mind fills with ideas of strong consequence for student misbehaviour and she chooses one.

"Please leave the classroom, Jacky."

Jacky stares back at her, but he does not move a muscle.

"Please leave the classroom!"

Daisy's face flushes with anger as she reaches out for his hair unable to control her hand and pulls on it. At the same time, she hears the collective moan of his fellow students and instinctively lets him go, her mind racing with words that can only formulate please forgive me, for I don't know what to do. Jacky lifts himself from his wooden bench and stomps loudly to the door, grabs the door handle, swings it open, climbs through the door frame and slams the door behind him. The curtain on the window flutters open to expose the angry expression of a young Chinese boy. Daisy doesn't look his way and walks to the front of the room and continues with her explanation of the lesson plan. Suddenly, there's a loud crash and the door swings open to expose Jacky standing in the door frame, his hands on his hips, his nostrils flared and his face red with anger. Daisy swallows bile and quickly looks around the room to locate Duan hua, the class Monitor and perceived assistant.

"Please go get Zhang Yu Ping and bring her here," Daisy commands. Zhang Yu Ping is the Foreign Affairs Director and the person who Daisy believes is the only person who can help squelch the class discipline problems that plague her at this Number One Senior Middle School in China. To her horror, the student does not move a muscle and Daisy feels the sting of the students' eyes on her and counts to herself to help hold back her tears. Oh my God, what have I done? What do I want? What can I do? To Daisy's great relief, the second Monitor stands and reports that she will go and get Zhang Yu Ping. Daisy feels grateful but cannot speak. Within minutes Wang Zhu appears at the door to see Daisy sitting on the raised floor at the front of the classroom. It is three fifty-six in the afternoon, Beijing Time, and everyone in the room is in the middle of a sit-in protest.

FROM THE JOURNAL OF A TESOL TEACHER

Perhaps you know me? I'm the guy who attends the company ESL training seminar before I head off to a teaching assignment in China.

My name is Dan, and it's my first time in China and my first attempt at teaching English as a second language in China. I'm excited the first day and enjoy the speakers but not the Chinese food. I dutifully attend the second day of the seminar feigning excitement and fighting back fear of the unknown. I accept my placement at a senior middle school in an obscure province and board the train with my luggage and one other workmate. I keep scratchy notes of the sights and sounds and things that are strange for me in China. My journal book becomes my best friend and constant travel companion. I report everything to my journal including the events that take place within the first few months of my teaching English in China. I leave it to you to decide why I pack up my suitcase and leave China without a goodbye to my colleague or employer and without a paycheque in that second month of the first semester. I leave it to you to read through my journal to find the incidents that pushed me so close to the edge that my only alternative was a midnight run.

Wednesday, Sept 6, Class 27
Introductions use family, hobbies and future bubble sheets. 56 students, 11 with English names – the rest I can't pronounce. We decided on the class conduct rules. Asked them to have an English notebook next class. 7 kids didn't hand in bubble sheet – ask for them next class.

Thursday, Sept 7, Class 28
English Bee questions and Free Talk. Didn't know what 'alphabet', 'vowel', 'consonant' meant = 3 new vocabulary words. 13 students with English notebooks. Students not familiar with free talk – keep it.

Wednesday, Sept 13, Class 29
Vocabulary Scramble and Bingo! and Free Talk - 17 with English notebook. Had to ask several students to stop talking and took the head phones from 8 students.

Thursday, Sept 14, Class 27

Music and song lyrics, questions about song and Free Talk. collected notebooks. 21 students handed in notebooks. Students not participating!

Wed, Sept 20, Class 28

Student one-on-one interviews, vocabulary, Free Talk Had time for 17 students, "Tell me about yourself", word search for rest of students. Only 7 students handed in vocabulary word search.

Thurs, Sept 21, Class 29

Vocabulary review and synonym challenge, hand in for marking. FAILURE! they don't know what synonyms are? SUCCESS! Taught them about synonyms.

Wed, Sept 27, Class 27

Synonym pop quiz, synonym challenge game and Free Talk. Too noisy! Had to stop and talk to 9 students, recorded their names but don't know what to do with their names. Who do I talk to?

Thurs, Sep 28, Class 28

Talk-About Box presentations and Free Talk. Thirteen sleeping, two sharing a music head set, seven missing what's with this class? Talk to other foreign teachers. What's Sam doing?

"Have you ever heard the term spat the dummy?" Sam says through a lisp that spews saliva, and then taking a queue from Dan, continues. "Well, in Australia, we use it to tell what happens when a baby screams, and the dummy, you know, the plug, or what do you Canadians call it? comes out of his mouth."

Sam Bullock titles himself a senior ESL instructor and has taught English in China for three years. The most remarkable thing about Sam is his shiny bald head which sports his tobacco stained moustache and goatee.

"We Canadians call it a pacifier."

"Yah, well, that's what I do with my class. I spit the dummy at the little buggers. I bang the desk sometimes, or crack my fist on the side of it. That keeps 'em on their toes 'cause then they don't know what I'll do next."

Dan nods his head but doesn't perform his eye-rolling action so that he hides his *oh, I can hardly wait to use his technique*, from their face-to-face conversation. Dan smiles and leaves Sam in the teacher's office. Much to Dan's horror, Sam's spit-the-dummy routine soon becomes part of his own.

Wed, Oct 1, Class 29
Word scramble with travel vocabulary and travel talk-about. Computer didn't work. Handed out postcards. Asked for written work on postcards. 37 students handed in their work. Improvement!

Thurs, Oct 2, Class 27
Wrote "Good Work" on overhead with 17 student's names. Travel vocabulary quiz and travel presentations. Free Talk.

Wed, Oct 11, Class 28
Arrive at class and it's cancelled. Do I detect glee?

Thurs, Oct 12, Class 29
Talk-about box and Free Talk. The overhead projector didn't work. Played the Travel Destination Railroad game. Free talk was interesting about Canada high schools versus Chinese high schools. Kid's liked it.

Wed, Oct 18, Class 27
Movie clip, questions and written answers. Had to stop video 3 times because kids talking, Leo, Gui Han Yu, Robing, Wang Shuyang, Crystal, Leng Qiang names to bring to Head Teacher.

"Thank you for meeting with me, Li Ying."

Li Ying is the Master Teacher for seven of the senior two international co-operative classes at this provincial number one high school and she doesn't speak a word of English. It's got to be a tough job by the looks of her. She wears her hair common enough with its communist dictated style pulled back in a tight pony tail projecting the face of a fifty-year old. She sports a navy blue blazer and a crisp white blouse this morning, with a man's red tie splitting the open jacket. She reaches over her desk to offer her hand and presents her long unadorned fingers and cut-to-the-quick fingernails. She doesn't smile but waves her left hand for Dan to sit, as she releases her grip of his hand.

"What is the problem, Dan?" Gui Yuan says.

Gui Yuan is the interpreter at this meeting and the Chinese English teacher who shares Class 27 with Dan. She's asked the foreign teachers to call her Lily. Without knowing it Dan has insulted Lily or as the Chinese refer to it caused face for her, a fact later revealed to Dan by Karen, a co-worker who is also teaching at this high school.

"You caused a problem because first, you couldn't solve the problem yourself, and then you got Lily involved and then you asked for a meeting with the Master Teacher. Ouch for Lily who I guess couldn't help you solve the class 27 problem and now you're asking to talk to the Head Teacher. This much attention to yourself can get you kicked out," Karen tells Dan and then shakes her head.

But Dan's decided to plough through with the meeting regardless of Chinese face. In Dan's opinion, the class is grossly misbehaved and it's got to be dealt with. Dan turns to Lily. "I've prepared a list of six students who interrupted the Wednesday class so much so that we couldn't complete the task. Please tell her that," Dan says, pointing to Li Ying, watching as Lily and Li Ying banter back and forth in a language he doesn't speak or understand and then Lily looks at him.

"The Master Teacher says that she will get the students to write you a note."

"What kind of note?"

"A letter of apologizing for their behaviour."

The room fills with Li Ying's chatter and her flipping up and down hand motion.

"The Master Teacher says this meeting is over."

"Over? What are the consequences for the students? I'd like to have her speak to them. Will she do that and ask them to be quiet in my class?"

"Yes, the Master Teacher is very busy, but she will do that," Lily says, and lifts herself up from the leather sofa, takes Dan's arm and leads him through the door.

> Dear Dan,
> This day, we make you unhappy in our class. We are wrong. We promise that we will be quiet and listen to you carefully. Please give us a chance. We will never do it again. If someone makes noise. Our monitor will take him(her) out. Please forgive us.
> Sincerely Yours, Class 27

Thu, Oct 19, Class 28
Travel word quiz, 'Going Places' travel in China pair work. Made an amazing discovery about MONITORS, there are two of them! and one English Study Leader and 4 group leaders. Now if I can get them on my side…

Wed, Oct 25, Class 29
What is your opinion? Questions about a song and the lyrics. Yikes! The class rebelled and refused to answer questions. No one said a word except to tell others in Chinese not to answer me. I SPAT THE DUMMY! Told them they didn't deserve me and walked out. What now? Who apologizes this time?

Thurs, Oct 26, Class 27
Rhyming words quiz and rap contest. Gathered 14 names on list of talkers, sleepers, 9 had headphones. Asked Monitors to help with keeping class quiet…worked for a few seconds. they're a combination

of false beginner, beginners and 5 of them are beginner-intermediate and their discipline is a combination of deplorable and horrible!

At 15:15 hours, Thursday, October 26, Dan meets Bill in the foreign teacher's office.

"Hi, Dan, how are you doing with your classes?"

"I just finished with class 27. They're a ripe bunch aren't they?"

"Yah, I see them twice a week too and they definitely can be a tough crowd. I heard you spit the dummy at them."

"Mmm, I never though I'd resort to Australian methodology."

"Yah, these kids are from wealthy parents and they don't know English, or at least most of them don't. So, I just ignore the ones that aren't listening and teach to the ones that at least look back at me when I look at them," Bill says, throwing his head back and sending out a loud laugh.

Bill McGill is a tall ex-Olympian coach who now specializes in teaching English as a second language to students in this high school in China. He speaks in a loud voice which he developed over many years of hollering at the athletes on the track and field.

"You can't do anything to make them listen. You just have to keep going for your forty minutes and then the class is over. Besides, you're just a token foreigner in this school. You're here to show that the school has foreigners. The government pays for the school to have foreigners and we're them. Don't think for a minute that anything you do in the class is of any value. I learned that the first year I was here by talking to the Chinese English teachers about our co-operative classes and even the public classes. Don't sweat it so much. Just go to class, teach for forty minutes and leave," Bill says.

His words swirl and swoosh in Dan's head. Dan's ears are pounding like drums – Bill's words have no place to go. Their ten minute break ends and they part ways to attend to their students.

Wed, Nov 1, Class 29

Writing dialogue using pictures, presenting conversation and free talk. Got through 7 pairs of students. No one handed in their work. I'll talk to Shen Cheng.

Shen Cheng is the academic assistant and sometime interpreter for Ms. Long, the Administrator of the Foreign Affairs Department at this high school. Shen Cheng's responsibility is to communicate with the foreign teachers on matters dealing with class schedules and student behaviour. Here are the emails Dan and he exchanged regarding Class 29.

> *Hello Shen Cheng,*
>
> *I wish to follow up on the conversation I had with you today about the discipline technique for students who choose to speak out of turn in Class 29. As I explained to you, my approach is to first speak to the student privately and tell them that their speaking out of turn behaviour is not acceptable and that my speaking to them now is their first warning. Next, I ask the student to stand. Finally, I ask the student to leave the classroom. The student is not allowed to return to my class until he or she has spoken to the Chinese English teacher and receives a note from that teacher, in English, that says they've talked about the issue and they have both signed it. I hope that this technique will encourage the student to look closely at his or her behaviour and possibly correct it. Thanks for your assistance, Regards, Dan*
>
> *Dear Dan,*
>
> *About the confirmation. I know you do this for all the students. But you'd better don't let the students go out of the classroom, just ask the student to stand in his seat, or stand in the back of the classroom. And if he still make noise you can send the student to the headmaster of the class, or get touch with the Chinese English teacher and discuss the way to solve the problem, because the teacher is more understanding the students, and maybe he or she can find the right way to help the student correct their wrong behavior. yours, Shen Cheng (Benz)*

> *Dear Benz,*
>
> *I am prepared to comply with your wish of keeping troublesome students in the classroom. Would you and the school administration consider having a different seating arrangement for the troublesome students. For example, there are two troublesome students that sit in the second row from the window in the back of the classroom. The name of one of the boys is Fu Cheng Zhi, but I do not know the name of the other boy. So, if Fu Cheng Zhi can be placed in the front of the classroom and away from the other boy it would be of great assistance to the rest of the students in the class who want to learn English. I would appreciate your considering this idea and returning my email with administration approval and implementation of this idea. Respectfully submitted, Dan*

Wednesday, November 8, lives in Dan's memory as the calm before the storm. Benz delivers a hand-written note from Yu Yan, the Chinese English teacher for Class 29. Benz reads it out loud to him and then places it in his hand and tells Dan that he can try to make his task easier by attracting the attention of the students. Dan looks at Benz but does not say a word. Within a few hours the following email appears on Dan's computer.

> *Dear Daniel,*
>
> *I've already spoken to him (Fu Cheng Zhi) in Class 29, Grade One. He has known that he is wrong. He said he was sorry to make you angry. And he promised me that he'll say sorry to you. I hope you can give him another chance. By the way, I want you to know something about class 29. They're a special group. They are not always behaving themselves in class, even in their head-teacher's class and mine. In common with you sometimes we also get cross. You can try to make your task easier for them to attract their attention. You may leave me a message when you have trouble, and I'll try to help you. Yu Yan, Class 29*

Dan made his midnight run from China on Thursday, November 10.

THE F*** YOU MESSAGE

Susan waves her arm over her head, catching the attention of her fellow English teacher and runs to him. She begs Andy to return to the classroom with her.

"What's wrong?" Andy says, as they trot down the hall in a school in China. Susan trusts Andy's skills as a teacher and considers him a friend. Susan's eyes flood with tears and a thickness forms in her throat.

"The students wrote something on the blackboard and I can't go back in there," she says, keeping her eyes forward.

Andy looks at Susan with concern and says, "What is it?"

Susan stops abruptly, leans up and out of breath whispers the profane message in his ear.

"You're kidding! That's awful."

They arrive at the entrance to the classroom and step over the threshold together. Every word that Susan saw on the blackboard only moments before is smeared away and only chalk dust remains.

"Who erased the blackboard?" Susan says to her audience of fifty-nine students. The students sit silent, staring straight ahead at the chalky blackboard.

"So, you're all denying any of you had anything to do with it?" Susan says, her eyes darting around the room and then she shouts, "You're all lying to me!" She holds her breath and steps back into the hallway with Andy.

"What would you do?" she asks him.

"Well, you have two choices. You can go back in there and carry on with your lesson like nothing happened, or," he pauses, "tell administration."

Susan blinks and watches as he turns and walks back down the hallway. Andy stops, turns to Susan and shouts, "Good luck with that. I've got to get to my class."

Susan holds her eyes shut as Andy disappears around the corner.

When she opens her eyes, the Master Teacher, Pei Mi, appears in the distance. The Master Teacher walks with a determined trot and stops abruptly in front of her. The women exchange smiles.

"How can I help you?" Pei Mi says. "Andy told me to come and talk with you."

Susan replies, "Well, it's awful. When I arrived at my classroom there was f*** you written on the blackboard," Susan blurts, and waits for a response but none appears on Pei Mi's face and nothing comes from her mouth. Susan continues, "My previous lesson was there too and all my questions for the class and right in the middle of it was… well you know. They've erased everything."

Pei Mi offers no response so Susan continues and hears her voice getting louder, "I'm shocked and horrified. I can't go back into a class where I'm not wanted. I'm sick about it. You'll have to get someone else to teach this class." It's difficult for her to continue because she doesn't what else to say and besides, she's changed her mind. "They are just children and sometimes they make mistakes," she says with a calm voice. Susan feels cold and lonely but knows she isn't alone and says, in a low, slow voice, "I'll talk to the students. Thanks for coming to see me." Susan turns from Pei Mi and enters the classroom, her head filled with the prayers she uses often to bring her back to the students. The case of the *f*** you* message was never solved, but in today's teaching world it's nice to know you're not alone. Susan's experience offers convincing evidence that this type of corrupt language, although acceptable in some circles, can be laid to rest as in the words of Abdu'l-Baha, *Were there no educators, all souls would remain savage, and were it not for the teacher, the children would be ignorant creatures.*

PURGED IN CHINA

Little did Frank know as he entered the room what he was about to discover. All at once he feels a surge of excitement at the scene of eighty academic strangers talking excitedly to one another, a rush of apprehension and a premonition of an extraordinary catastrophe in this new world. He is greeted first by a tall woman with an Australian accent and then by a young round-faced American who tells him that she will be his teaching partner. Frank is guided to an empty chair by Margaret and Christine and invited to join them. He can't shake his apprehension and chalks it up to a combination of limited experience teaching English as a second language and culture change in China. One other thing rings true for Frank today - he's unaccustomed to working in a team. He's sixty-two years old with forty-seven years work experience most of it spent independently.

The first person to start unravelling Frank's teaching experience in China is Margaret, when she asks how long he'd been doing it. Frank looks at Margaret and hesitates for a moment, apprehensive about revealing even a nugget about his past, present or future, and then says, "I taught students for three weeks at the end of my six-month TESOL course, but that's it."

He looks at Margaret for a reaction but only hears her say that she took a three-day course and now she's here. Christine chirps that she is a teacher with credentials from a university in America and has taught kindergarten and knows all about the curriculum statements and lesson planning that the director is speaking about. All three turn to see the academic director clapping her hands and pointing to the door and hear her telling the audience to go out to start their lesson planning. Frank scoops up his papers and follows Christine to a classroom filled with desks and wooden stools. Christine perches herself on one of the stools, takes out her music-player earplugs and stuffs them into her ears – a do not disturb sign. Frank stands looking at her as she opens her notebook, locates something in one of the many seminar handouts and begins writing. Frank sits on a stool next to her but does not want to interrupt her. He doesn't want to ask, what are we doing? Frank can't recall ever asking that question and wasn't about to start now. For the next forty minutes, Frank sits quietly flipping through his papers hiding his feelings of deliberately being ignored by Christine. There is a knock on the classroom door and Frank and Christine are asked to return to the main meeting room. In the meeting room all teachers are directed to board the busses which will eventually take them to their teaching locations.

Frank, Margaret and Christine arrive at Yichang No.1 High School and meet with the Cai Rui Zin, Director of Foreign Language Teaching Department. Frank's intuition, his premonition of an extraordinary catastrophe is heightened as he shakes hands with him. Margaret strategically jockeys for leadership position by negotiating a start date for the team and guarantees the production of weekly lesson plans to be delivered to the inbox of Cai Rue Zin. The first lesson plan for Frank and Christine as a teaching team is the end of lesson planning for Frank. Christine's reaction to Frank's ideas is that they are wrong and she tells him, 'this is how we do it in America'. So, Frank decides that he will leave the entire lesson planning to Christine. Over the next three months Christine feels overwhelmed with doing all the lesson plans and her rage with this task boils over and results in a letter to company headquarters. Nancy, the Academic and Human Resources Manager arranges an emergency meeting with the team and listens to Margaret report on Frank's attitude toward the students.

Margaret points to Frank across the meeting table and says to Nancy, "He's out of control. He told us at one of the team meetings that he wasn't able to control the students because they were talking to each other and so his choice, if you can believe it, was to lift up one of the desks and slam it down."

Frank looks over at Margaret and then at Christine as they stare back at him. Frank feels content that his intuition is correct about the impending disaster and realizes that it isn't banging the desk in the classroom that is at issue here, it's that Margaret and Christine want him out and this is what it takes to get him out – tattling out of school. Frank recalls that his desk banging incident had a very noisy beginning in his classroom. As his fifty-nine students shouted and tossed things around the room, his classroom monitor was pleading with him in her soft voice, "Mr. Black, you need to keep the students quiet. You can do move the difficult students to different seats so that they don't talk to their friends." Frank took her advice and began sorting the difficult students in and amongst the quiet, dedicated ones. However, one student told him that he would not move. Frank's reaction to being defied by a youngster was to lift the desk up and move it for him, banging it down hard where it was meant to be. The crash put a halt to all conversation and the lesson continued. Frank reported all this detail to the team members much to his regret. The mysterious impending disaster Frank projected the first time he laid eyes on Margaret and Christine turned itself into an open far-off success in which Frank ends up surrounded by young, enthusiastic junior middle school students. But the foreboding feeling never leaves Frank and it precedes him to his new school.

At the new school in Jiang Su province, Frank meets a teacher named Sally. Sally's job includes communicating what is needed by the Chinese school Director of Foreign Assisted Studies to the contracted teachers and also observing the conduct of the foreign teachers in the classroom. Sally introduces Frank to Jale, the Director of Foreign Assisted Studies at a 'meet and greet' dinner. Sally gets so drunk that the teaching team has to pour her into a taxi and send her home. From her conduct it seemed to Frank that her world was viewed through a haze of cigarette smoke and the bottom of her glass. At the time, Frank thought, hmmm, this is our leader? Time did not change much of his impression. Sally made it quite clear to Frank the first time they spoke about teaching attire that short pants, knee-high socks, and kilts especially, were not appropriate. When Sally made mention of the phrase, *when in Rome*, Frank retorted that he wasn't in Rome and that his culture had a place in the world also. The purge was set in motion. The purge process presented itself again one day as Frank was walking into town and met Jale, who stopped in front of him straddling her bicycle. The brief conversation was friendly but Frank didn't doubt his feelings of anticipating the worst. The next morning Frank received an email:

> *Frank, I am told you were wearing "a dress" in town yesterday. I know it is a kilt but the chinese don't. The school here would appreciate your not wearing this style in public as they feel it draws undue attention to us and to them. I haven't informed you before as I was hoping this would not arise but that is their ruling. Please adhere to their wishes on this matter. Sally*

The next day, Sally kept her promise to Frank that she and Jale would drop in to observe one of his classes and she couldn't have picked a better class to gather information for the ultimate purge of Frank from the school. Frank's Class 4 was a sometimes unruly bunch of students and a tough crowd to keep one hundred percent engaged. Sally and Jale entered Frank's classroom unannounced and sat on stools at the back of the room, clasping onto their clipboards and scratching copious notes as they bobbed their heads in unison, up to view Frank, down to the paper. The room charged with negative energy emanating from the observers and the observed. Several days later, Frank was summoned to meet privately with Sally and Jale. Lieutenant Sally and Major Jale, as Frank envisioned them, sat stiff-backed facing him. He imagined both women dressed in green fatigues sporting the distinctive red star. The speech by Jale was fast and furious and filled with threatening tones. Frank sat quietly, solemnly, listening carefully to his final purge.

Wenbi Tower, Changzhou

VII

Teaching Group Work in China: A Real-Life Lesson Plan

> The nice thing about teamwork is that you always have others on your side.
> - Margaret Carty

Research published by Gavin Melles at Melbourne University in Australia, on the topic of Asian attitude toward working in groups, says that Asian learners prefer more collaborative and group learning and that group work is aimed at helping them learn how to work with other people and deal with different views, different opinions. Melles's research explores the way students account for their experience in group work and finds student perception regarding the benefits and challenges of group work appears to play a diverse and sometimes unexpected role in their experience that they tend to instinctively assist each other once they understand the collective purpose of a group.

In the twenty-two years I've spent developing and implementing group work lesson plans in both the western hemisphere and in China, my observations have been that the students showed diversity only after having been taught the collective purpose of a group and how to conduct themselves in it. Once the participants are elected into a position or are assigned duty roles they recognize and understand the united purpose of their group. Most of my Canadian students initially resisted the temptation to help one another because of the view held by them that what they produce at school is exclusively theirs to submit for a reward or a grade. Only after they were advised that a group mark would be given did the students lean toward helping each other. In China, it's been my observation that students assist each other by whispering answers and support to others in the group only after having been given permission to do so or encouraged to conduct themselves that way.

Melles's research also says that when questioned about their experience, the majority of the students admitted that group work helped them improve their listening skills and leadership skills by first co-operatively developing the team rules and then encouraging each other to use them. In my classes in China, the students said that group work helps them assist other group members to overcome their shyness and contribute freely without prejudice.

If guided gently when working in groups, students learn how to deal with different views and accept different opinions and remain unrestrained while presenting their own ideas. Group work is not instinctive and therefore it has to be learned. Working within a group is a challenging and interesting process that brings personal opinion, prejudice and don't-care attitudes together. What is instinctive is the tendency to protect yourself and your ideas. In this way the Chinese student is no different from any other who has never learned to work in a group. In a five member group, the Chinese student is given opportunities to act as Monitor, Writer, Speaker, Timekeeper, and Assistant. Young people like to take on responsibilities and allocating jobs to students according to their abilities is always a successful way of rewarding them.

Runyi Chen, School of Foreign Studies, South China Normal University and Bernard Hird Edith, Cowan University, Australia, write in *Group Work in the EFL Classroom in China: A Closer Look*:

> Small group work in an English as a Foreign Language classroom has been largely accepted as an effective strategy in the development of students' communicative proficiency in English. This acceptance has occurred despite a lack of research in key areas about what actually happens when students work in groups in real classrooms. Chen and Edith's study examines both quantitative and qualitative data relating to student behaviour in groups collected in EFL lessons in China. Tape recordings of group discussions were analysed and data dealing with turn taking and length of turns were calculated. Interview data were also collected and student perceptions of their contributions to the discussions are presented. Results highlight the complexity of what happens when students work in groups in EFL lessons. The study also states that it is difficult to generalize about student behaviour in group work and though there are some aspects of how students behave in groups that are well understood, there are still many questions that remain unexplored regarding how group work functions in the EFL setting.

One of the most pressing questions is: How Can a TESOL Teacher Make Group Work Work?' In my communications with Runyi Chen, I offered to take up the challenge of preparing, executing and writing about a series of steps to teach students how to conduct themselves in groups and with his encouragement it came to fruition. In this case, you will be part of the ongoing research if you choose to use the steps because you are welcome to contact me with your findings. You can use this powerful tool to help your students improve their English language communication skills and guide them to discuss with one another rather than impose as it should be with consultation. John Kolstoe, in his Baha'i Consultation Workbook, writes:

> *Consultation is a process of sharing thoughts and feelings through talking things out in an atmosphere of love and harmony with a commitment to accomplish some definite, common purpose. Consultation is a means of using the power of cooperation and unity in groups. Two or more people, working together, can have a power, wisdom, and insight far beyond what those same people have as individuals.*

Students who participate in group work are guided to respect each member of their group by submissive behaviour, and refrain from chatting on excessive and unrelated matters. Students are directed to act out meeting conditions that include respect, honesty, openness, courtesy, dignity, care and moderation and are lead to understand the pleasure of expressing an opinion without belittlement from another group member. Students learn to use co-operative learning methods because of its strong importance as a requirement of future employment. Some of my students, as young as fourteen, in China, when asked about how learning affects their future, tend to answer with 'make lots of money', 'be a boss', 'be a famous superstar', and 'be rich'. These students demonstrate a strong tendency towards instrumental motivation to inspire the goal to gain some social or economical reward through learning a second language. The teacher's task is to provide an avenue for language learning in a group setting and to help the learner achieve high levels of integrative motivation which is characterized by the learner's positive attitudes towards the target language and the desire to integrate into the target language. In the case of most Chinese students, money makes their world go around and this global phenomenon can be used to your advantage and their reward as you teach them how to work in groups in a classroom setting.

In western culture, most employers are no longer looking for graduates with the highest academic results, but for team leaders and players who can work with others for the common good of all. This influence can be felt in some of the organizations that have chosen to operate here in China. Unfortunately, many of the high achievers in academic institutions are very competitive individuals and find it difficult to work with others in groups. Hence the importance of teaching group work in such a setting is to encourage co-operative learning.

GROUP WORK IS THE WORK OF THE DEVIL

"For the life of me, I can't understand why you want to have the students work in groups. Group work in a Chinese classroom is the work of the devil. I avoid it like the plague because I have to keep interrupting the students from chatting with each other in Chinese. And they don't know what to do in a group," declares Michelle Landon.

Michelle is a colleague in China and her comments represent eighty-six percent of the seventy-two teachers both native speakers and Chinese that I've spoken to in the last three years. Generally the comments about group work included statements like you can't teach students who don't listen, they're distracted with each other when they sit facing each other in groups, they talk Chinese in groups, groups are too much work, and they don't know what group work is. All of these comments are valid but it's not impossible to teach group work in China and it's far easier than working with rows and rows of students. What makes it so easy is that you are now armed with knowledge of the communist structure in the classroom and you can assign a role to specific students in the group or you can demonstrate a more democratic environment by inviting the students to select their own group Monitor, Writer, Speaker, Timekeeper, and Assistant.

Often a teacher in Canada assumes that students know intuitively or have received instruction elsewhere on the process of working with others in a group, whereas this is not necessarily the case. The same holds true for students in a classroom in China. The result of such an assumption in either culture can range from personal conflict between members to a poorly executed group to one or a few members taking responsibility for the project.

WHAT IS A GROUP?

The first step in establishing a classroom group mentality for your Chinese learners is to encourage the students to consider the entire class as a group by asking, *What is a group?* By using mind-mapping and brainstorming techniques, you can elicit and cluster the students' ideas and help them learn what a group means. At this point, if you have access to multi-media equipment it would be beneficial to show the dynamics of a group sport like their beloved basketball players engaged in a match. Chinese boys love basketball because it makes them strong and healthy and the young Chinese girls love strong, healthy boys. It's an important first-step in the foundation of establishing a team vision of how they would like to proceed, what they would like their responsibilities to be, what is their understanding of the nature of the assignment, and what are their expectations of their group members? This first simple question can be the discussion prompter that your students need about the workings of a group in advance of the experience and will more likely result in an experience for members that enhances individual group skills as well as resulting in a more desirable group product and learning experience.

YOUR JOB AS PROJECT MANAGER

Your job as Project Manager is to determine the start up tasks and issues that will result in the best experience for the group in carrying out the assigned project. For some classroom applications an educational goal is learning to work as a group; in other instances the goal is connected more closely to a specific assignment and the group process is of secondary importance. A list of possible start up tasks is provided under "Teaching Group Work Instructions", however, these can be modified to fit specific classroom needs. As Project Manager, you should hold students accountable for completing the start up tasks and for proceeding with their group work in a manner consistent with the decisions they made during the discussion of start up tasks. For example, group conduct rules that are generated during this discussion should be agreed upon by all the members and be enforced during the group project. Student accountability can be determined in a number of ways: (1) students can summarize the decisions they have made in a brief presentation to their classmates; (2) handouts can have questions that ask students to assess various aspects of their group process; (3) the Project Manager can hold regular or unscheduled meetings with groups to attain a sense of the group experience for participants.

TEACHING GROUP WORK INSTRUCTIONS

Group formation in China is the same as in Canada. For example, in Canada students tend to sit in the same seat throughout the semester that they occupied on the first day of class. When classes are homogenous, it may be simply a matter of keeping one's initial territory staked out. In China, students do not always have the privilege of sitting where they want because the tendency is that the Chinese English teacher dictates where her students will sit and sometimes the Head Teacher in charge of all the senior one, two and three teachers will dictate who sits where in a classroom. If you happen to share a classroom with a like-minded foreign teacher you can provide the students the enjoyment of sitting in a classroom that is configured in group formation to encourage a group culture. The Chinese teaching system dictates that the students sit in rows. So, if you find yourself in a classroom that is configured in rows, the students can be introduced to forming a group in their area.

In Canada, forming a group on the basis of language encourages students to use their native language instead of the target language. In China, it is the same and so you must also be able to engage group participants so that they are encouraged to speak, read, write and listen in English. Canadian students tend to form groups with friends rather than on the basis of complementary abilities that may be more useful for learning. In China, especially if you offer up a room with empty desks clustered in group formation, the students will form groups with friends. The following list is a guide to help you teach group work.

1. Students should be organized into groups. Groups can be designated in a variety of ways: (a) by random process; (b) by student's common interests or concerns; (c) assign students to specific groups based on various individual characteristics. The size of the group is dependent on the group task. Groups can be just about any size starting with two to three members. For most group projects, five members work well. An odd number of members also ensure that members will not create ties in decision making.
2. Students should be given the assignment they will work on as a group.
3. Prior to the start of the assignment, they should be given a list of start up tasks and instructed to discuss the start up tasks. Typical start up tasks that students might discuss are:
    a Introduce the concept of a group by asking the question: What is a group?
    b Designate one person to begin to monitor the group and other members to act as writer, speaker, timekeeper, and assistant.

c   Generate a list of ground rules that will help the group achieve a group culture. Typical areas to include in ground rules are: (1) participation and assuming responsibilities; (2) contributing communication courtesies; (3) methods to be made in decision making.
d   Select a group name.
e   Discuss the group assignment and prepare a list of questions.
f   Prepare a timeline to follow to complete the assignment.
g   Help the writer prepare a briefing to the class about the key decisions that have been made during the start up task discussion.

The start up process cannot be ignored and should be visited regularly to remind the students of its significance every time they engage in a group activity. You can encourage cooperation in a group by letting the group develop its personality as the semester continues.

In China, the role of classroom Monitor is to observe and report the overall conduct of the students in the class and so this assignment of duty to the group is not much different. The group Monitor, with encouragement to promote a consultative approach, can direct the group to perform its duty as a whole by guarding the ground rules as decided upon by the entire membership. The group Monitor can also encourage participation by supporting the Timekeeper in her duty to track speaking and presentation time. At the same time, the Project Manager encourages and promotes participation by all group members by ensuring that each person has a job to perform.

With regard to communication courtesy, it can be promoted as a general classroom courtesy such as: *Don't talk when someone else is talking.* As Project Manager you can track who is performing what duty and at the beginning of the next project you might like to promote the rotation of duty. When it comes to group decision making, the most conducive method is open, unobstructed participation and contribution of ideas. A never-fail technique is the "Chinese-Save-Face-Scrap-Paper Method" (I made up the name). It works by having all contributions made by group members in writing using scrap paper which virtually obliterates peer pressure and the face condition often associated with Chinese culture, although in China the youth tend not to factor in face so much as keeping their territory staked out, as is common with narcissist behaviour.

Members of a group whose atmosphere is clearly defined as a place to share ideas without prejudice or harassment equal the *matching social relational model*, where each member is encouraged to contribute to the value of the group and a 100% consensus is sought after but not always achieved and in that case the majority rules. Group work supports the use of co-operative learning, in which students have different tasks and must share their skills, ideas, decisions and results with team members in order to complete the assigned project.

Canadian students have an expectation that their school work and also group work will contribute to a final mark. In China, there is no such expectation from either the Chinese teacher or the students. The value students assign to group work is strictly economical in that they anticipate that learning English will contribute to a high paying job. Based on this fact, you will be successful in teaching group work if you promote it as a necessary tool for the success they so keenly desire.

In Canada, when a social relational model is violated, discomfort and sanctions can occur. For example, a student who is uncomfortable with the other group members may have the luxury of complaining to her teacher and that teacher has the authority and skill to reassign the student or encourage the student to form her own group. In China, it is unlikely that a student would complain to you or express any discomfort with her group members. In any situation, the ever perceptive Project Manager keeps an eye and ear out for any discomfort or exclusion or group violations and formulates a solution that is conducive to the situation and to China's education system.

The group needs to be supported in identifying its *communal social relationship*, a social bond based on a common goal. Your students, like the rest of us, engage in an activity as much for the social relationships engendered as for the goal of the activity. We are by nature social beings.

THE STRUCTURE OF A FIVE MEMBER GROUP

The diagram below shows the structure of a five member group. Groups set up this way have potential for fun and present a clear idea of duty and responsibility for each member.

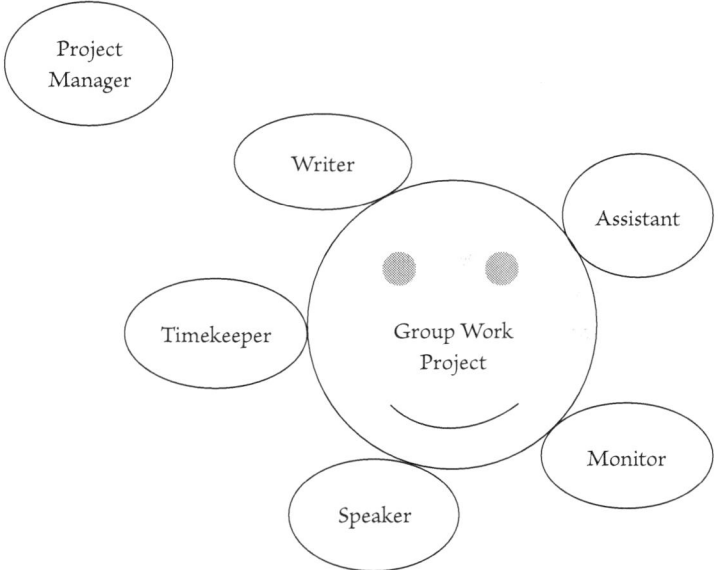

Figure 2: Structure of a Five Member Group

Cards showing group Monitor, Writer, Speaker, Timekeeper, and Assistant with a description and duty shown on the back are handed out in the *Start Up Task Activity* phase. Here are samples of group member's duty card:

Group Monitor: A Group Monitor is someone who helps guide correct and fair conduct. The duty of the Group Monitor is to be in charge of the ground rules and to ensure that other group members follow them. For example, if a member is talking out of turn, then the Monitor can help by gently asking the person to wait his turn to speak.

Writer: A Writer is someone who makes a record of something by writing it down. The duty of the Writer is to write down a summary that is spoken by each group member. The Writer can interrupt anytime to ensure accuracy and explaining. For example, the Writer can ask someone to repeat something in order to write it down correctly.

Speaker: A Speaker is somebody who talks for the group. The duty of the Speaker is to talk for the rest of the group members when presenting information. For example, after the group has made a final decision the Speaker tells the rest of the class about that decision.

Timekeeper: A Timekeeper is somebody who keeps track of the time spoken by each member of the group. The duty of the Timekeeper is to keep track of the time that the group spends on talking, decision making and making a presentation. For example, if the Project Manager assigns two minutes for the group to generate ideas, then the Timekeeper tells the group to stop after two minutes.

In the *Start Up Task Activity* phase of the Group Work Lesson Plan, there is opportunity for discussion on the concept of a group by asking the class What is a Group? The plan shows a brainstorm activity first to identifying synonyms for the word group and then to put the synonyms into context statements. In *Activity No. 1: True False Quiz*, students fill out a true/false quiz and then the answers are taken up with the whole class. This reinforces the student's understanding of group and group work. Then, in *Activity No. 2: Name Work Groups*, students are guided to come up with a name for their group. Next, in *Activity No. 3: Identify Membership*, students are given identity cards and asked to read them aloud to the entire class. Discussion and clarification are important at this point. Then, in *Activity No. 4: Group Ground Rules*, students are guided to generate a list of ground rules that will help them achieve a group culture. Next, in *Activity No. 5: Group Work Action*, students put into action what they've learned about groups and group work and apply his or her duty to the task of working within the group.

GROUP WORK LESSON PLAN

You will have best results if you organize your students in groups from the onset of this project. The plan is geared toward senior middle school students or young adults who are at a comprehension level of English of lower intermediate to intermediate. The methodology is a communicative approach which involves getting the students to use English in a group setting. The students are presented with many opportunities to speak to each other in their group, to others in other groups and to you. The resource materials utilize a student handout, an overhead projector, scrap paper, a digital video disk (DVD) player, a video display screen, and a dictionary and thesaurus. As you progress through the plans you will come up with clever and wonderful resource ideas of your own. The language skill objective is learning to work as a group.

<u>Start Up Task Activity: What is a group?</u>
Teacher displays a short video, with the sound turned off, of a basketball team engaged in a game. Teacher writes *What is a group?* on the blackboard as well as the following two statements:

> (A) A group of people is a number of people together in one place at one time. (B) A group of people is a set of people who have the same interests, and who organize themselves to work together.

Teacher reads sentences (A) and (B) to the class. The whole class is encouraged to chant each sentence. Then the English Study Leader reads each sentence and then each group chants each sentence.

<u>Teaching Task No.1: What is a Group?</u>
Teacher asks: *What is a group?* Students are encouraged to restate the (A) or (B) sentences. Teacher directs student attention to recall the basketball game video and asks: *Is a basketball team a group?* Students are encouraged to respond and explain their answer. Teacher reinforces phrases spoken in sentence (A) and (B) by encouraging students to familiarize themselves with concepts like "together in one place at one time" and "same interests" and "work together". Teacher asks: *Is your family a group? Is this class a group?* Students are encouraged to respond and explain their answer. Teacher validates all responses by summarizing and restating the (A) and (B) sentences.

<u>Teaching Task No.2: Synonyms for Group</u>
Teacher draws circle graph with five or more branches extending from it and writes *group* in the middle. The students are asked to use their thesaurus or dictionary and also brainstorm for synonyms.
<u>Vocabulary</u>: group, bunch, gang, pack, crowd, party, band

One student is asked to read sentence A and replace the word group with one of the synonyms. Another student is asked to read sentence B and replace group with one of the synonyms. All synonyms are used in place of the word group.

(A) A _____ of people is a number of people together in one place at one time. (B) A _____ of people is a set of people who have the same interests, and who organize themselves to work together.

Activity No. 1: Group True or False Quiz
Teacher provides each student with Group True or False Quiz handout. The students are given a few minutes to read through the questions and then either the teacher or the English Study Leader can read one sentence out loud but not give their answer. Afterward, the students are asked to work individually on the quiz.

What is a Group?
True or False Quiz

1. The students in this senior middle school are a group.   T   F
2. The teachers in this senior middle school are a group.   T   F
3. The students in senior one are a group.   T   F
4. The students in this classroom are a group.   T   F
5. The players in a basketball team are a group.   T   F
6. The people in your family are a group.   T   F
7. Group work sounds like fun.   T   F
8. A group of people is a number of people together in one place at one time.   T   F
9. A group is a set of people who have the same interests, and who organize themselves to work together.   T   F
10. We are going to learn how to work as a group this semester.   T   F

Teacher displays true/false statements on overhead project and individual students are asked to contribute their answers. Students correct their own work. All the answers are True.

THE LITTLE RED BOOK

Activity No. 2: Name Work Groups

Students are guided to come up with a group name and to record it and the membership names on a piece of scrap paper. One of the group members posts the group information on the blackboard. Afterward the teacher can assign duties to each member.

Activity No. 3: Identify Membership and Duty

Teacher displays the compiled group names and duty assignment on overhead. Teacher hands out a *Duty Card* to each group member. Each card shows the duty title and responsibility. Teacher calls out a duty and the responsible members are encouraged to read the description out loud. Students are encouraged to discuss how they can contribute to the group. Teacher supports the discussion by asking: Timekeeper, how can you help the group? Each duty is discussed.

Activity No. 4: Group Ground Rules

Teacher posts a few group ground rules on the blackboard to initiate discussion and to encourage the students to generate other rules that will help the group achieve a group culture. Areas to be covered are: (1) participation and assuming responsibilities; (2) contributing communication courtesies; (3) decision making.

- Actively listen – Please don't talk when someone else is talking
- Be prepared to do your duty as group Monitor, Writer, Speaker, Timekeeper, or Assistant.
- The group needs your ideas.
- All ideas are good ideas.
- Everyone decides on an idea.

Teacher guides students to brainstorm on ground rules for their group on scrap paper and then to post all ideas on the blackboard. All ideas are good ideas. Teacher collects all the scrap paper ideas and posts them in the classroom for all to see.

<u>Activity No. 5: Group Work Action</u>
One member of the group is secretly chosen by the other members of the group. Supply each group with a very large piece of paper, and several differently coloured pens. Then ask the students to describe the chosen member within the group by writing down adjectives on the paper. Firstly, ask the group to describe the chosen student physically, using just one colour of pen. Then get the group to ask the student questions about themselves in English. Ask them to record the answers in different colours – for example, 'likes' in green ink, and 'dislikes' in red. Next, ask the groups to come to the front of the classroom one by one. Pin up their large piece of paper, and ask the rest of the class to guess whom the group have been describing. If time allows, the class can ask the chosen members questions about what has been written. For example, if it has been written that the chosen member dislikes rain, ask why, and then ask the rest of the class to raise their hands if they agree or disagree. This exercise also has strong benefits regarding student bonding and contributes to the development of a group culture.

Bibliography

Ames, C., & Ames, R. (1989). Research in motivation in education (vol. 3). San Diego, CA: Academic Press.

Banya, K., & Chen, M. (1997). Beliefs about language learning: A study of beliefs of teachers' and students' cultural setting. Paper presented at the 31st Annual Meeting of the Teachers of Speakers of Other Languages, Florida.

Chawhan, L., & Oliver, R, (2000). What beliefs do ESL students hold about language learning? TESOL in Context, 10 (1), 20-26.

Chew, Phyllis G.L. The Chinese Religion and the Bahai Faith. Oxford. George Ronald, 1993

Horwitz, E.K. (1987). Surveying student beliefs about language learning. In A.L. Wenden 7 J. Robin (Eds.) Learner Strategies in Language Learning, (pp.119-132). London: Prentice Hall

Melles, G. (2004). Understanding the role of language/culture in group work through qualitative interviewing. The Qualitative Report, 9(2), 216-240. Retrieved [2006/12/22], from http://www.nova.edu/ssss/QR/QR9-2/melles.pdf

Wenden, A (1986). Helping language learners think about learning. English Language Teaching Journal, 40, 3-12.

ISBN 142515915-X

Made in the USA
Lexington, KY
01 February 2010